Second Edition

HOTEL ENGLISH

JAE-YEON YANG

BAEKSAN Publishing Co.

Hotel English

Preface

교통수단 및 기술의 발달과 여행의 대중화로 국가 간 문화의 장벽은 서서히 낮아지고 있지만 여전히 외국인 고객을 응대하는 데 필요한 언어의 장벽은 우리가 넘어야 할 중요한 과제 중 하나입니다. 각 나라마다 고유의 언어가 존재하고 일부 국가에서는 수십 개의 언어가 통용되기도 합니다. 서로 다른 언어를 구사하는 다양한 문화권의 사람들이 서로 교류하기 위해서는 누구와도 소통이 가능한 세계 공용어(公用語)가 필요하며 아직까지 모두가 공인하는 가장 영향력 있는 언어는 영어입니다. 실제로 전 세계에서 영어로 소통 가능한 인구가 약 15억 명 이상으로 추정된다는 재미있는 통계가 발표되기도 하였습니다.

이처럼 글로벌 역량의 기본은 영어이며, 그 가운데서도 호텔리어를 꿈꾸는 여러분에게 기본적인 영어 소통능력은 필수요소입니다. 호텔리어로서 영어로 외국인 고객들을 응대할 때 어렵고 현란하며 긴 호흡의 문장을 구사할 필요는 전혀 없습니다. 오히려 상대방이 이해하기 쉽게 간결한 문장과 표현을 사용하는 것이 효과적일 수 있습니다.

본 교재는 호텔리어를 꿈꾸는 전공자들을 위하여 호텔 각 부서별로 빈번하게 사용되는 표현들을 쉽게 이해하고 훈련할 수 있도록 구성하였습니다. 후반부로 진행될수록 상황별 표현법들에 공통적인 공식이 존재한다는 것을 깨달을 수 있을 것입니다. 문장의 뼈대가 되는 기본 패턴들을 이해하고 이 패턴들에 익숙해지면 그 이후에는 자유자재로 문장 확장이 가능해집니다. 이러한 훈련을 위하여 각 Unit마다 세부상황에 대한 대화내용들이 비교적 짧은 호흡으로 반복되므로 파트너와 함께 호텔리어와 고객의 역할놀이를 통하여 상황별 표현법들을 학습해 보기 바랍니다.

호텔에 도착하기 전 예약부터 호텔에 머물다가 호텔을 떠나는 순간에 이르기까지 시간 순서에 의하여 부서별로 Unit 구성을 하였으며, 본문의 이해를 돕고자 모든 Unit의 시작은 부서 소개와 직무에 대한 설명으로 시작합니다. 단원마다 평균적으로 약 5~7개의 Conversation 훈련을 마친 뒤 본문에서 다뤘던 내용 중에 더 구체적으로 이해하고 넘어갈 필요가 있는 정보들을 제공하고 있으며 마지막에는 우리가 잘 알고 있는 전 세계 호텔 브랜드들의 흥미로운 스토리들이 펼쳐집니다. 교재의 마지막 부분에는 호텔용어를 알파벳 순으로 정리하여 수록하였으니 미래의 호텔리어들에게 유용한 안내서가 되었으면 합니다.

이 책을 읽는 여러분 모두의 소중한 꿈을 응원하겠습니다.
끝으로 본 교재의 출간을 위하여 정성을 다해주신 백산출판사 관계자분들께 깊은 감사의 말씀을 드립니다.

2021년 1월
저자 양 제 연

Contents

Unit
05 Telephone Service — 73

Unit
06 Food and Beverage Service — 91

Unit 01

Reservations

We will learn
- how to take a reservation
- how to confirm the reservation
- how to deal with cancellation

Hotel English

1. What They Do

객실예약업무

객실예약은 객실을 이용하고자 하는 고객이 전화, 팩스, 여행사, 홈페이지, 직접 방문, 온라인 / 모바일 예약 대행업체 등 다양한 경로를 통하여 객실을 예약하는 것으로 호텔과 고객 간 관계가 형성되는 첫 번째 과정이라고 할 수 있습니다.

예약업무의 핵심은 친절하고 신속하며 정확한 업무수행에 있습니다. 또한 고객이 객실예약 이외에 다른 문의 사항이 있더라도 효과적으로 응대할 수 있도록 호텔 관련 정보 뿐 아니라 호텔 주변 관광지, 쇼핑, 레스토랑, 공연 및 축제 등 다양한 정보들을 숙지하고 있어야 합니다.

객실예약업무 시 확인해야 할 사항

- 투숙객 성명
- 투숙객 연락처
- 체크인 예정일
- 체크아웃 예정일
- 객실 종류 및 투숙인원수
- 지불방식
- 객실요금 및 통보 확인
- 고객의 요청 사항 확인
- 예약 번호 포함 예약 관련 모든 정보와 취소규정 등에 관한 안내

2. Conversations

Conversation 1 Taking Reservations

"Do you have any rooms available for tomorrow?"

Reservation: Good afternoon. Marriott Hotel reservations. How can I help you?

Guest: Do you have any rooms available for tomorrow?

Reservation: Yes, we do. What kind of room would you like?

Guest: I want a double room.

Reservation: Let me check. Fortunately, we have just one left.

Guest: That sounds great. What is the best rate you can offer?

Reservation: We can offer you our promotional weekend rate of $210 per night including breakfast.

Guest: Let me take it, so please reserve it for me. Put it under the name of Andrew Johnson.

Reservation: Mr. Johnson, could you give me a credit card number? I need it to guarantee the reservation.

Guest: Sure. It's a Visa card and the number is 8193-5212-9870-4731.

Reservation: Could you tell me the expiry date, please?

Guest: 10/21

Reservation: Thank you, Mr Johnson. Your reservation number is MH247GX. We look forward to seeing you tomorrow.

Guest: Thank you, bye.

Conversation 2 Handling Reservation Inquiries

"Could I have a room on a lower floor, please?"

Clara Good morning. Hilton Hotel Clara speaking.
How may I help you?

Guest Good morning. I'd like to make a reservation for a room.

Clara Yes, madam. When are you supposed to arrive?

Guest I'll be there on Friday, 23rd of March.

Clara How long are you going to stay?

Guest I will stay for two nights.

Clara You will check out on March 25th, won't you?

Guest Yes, that's right. Could I have a room on a lower floor, please?
I don't like using the lift.

Clara Is the second floor ok?

Guest Yes, that's perfect.

Clara May I have your name, please?

Guest It's Jennifer Lawrence.

Clara How do you spell your last name?

Guest It's L-A-W-R-E-N-C-E.

Clara How can we contact you, ma'am?

Guest You can reach me at 808-213-6904.

Clara All right, Ms. Lawrence. I'll see you on the 23rd of March.
Thank you for calling.

Guest Thank you. Goodbye.

Conversation 3 Making Suggestions

"But we have lots of rooms available for the next weekend."

Elena	Good afternoon. Park Hyatt Hotel. Elena speaking.
Guest	I'd like to book a room for three nights from the 15th of October.
Elena	I'm very sorry, we're fully booked on that day. You know Busan International Film Festival will begin on the 15th.
Guest	Oh, that's very disappointing.
Elena	But we have lots of rooms available for the next weekend.
Guest	Then I'll make a reservation for a deluxe double room for three nights starting on the 22nd of October. How much will the room cost?
Elena	It is $250 including tax and service charges.
Guest	Can I have a room with an ocean view?
Elena	I'm afraid that I can't guarantee a room with an ocean view. However, I'll make a special request to the front desk.
Guest	All right, thank you.
Elena	May I ask your name, please?
Guest	Emma Watson.
Elena	How can we contact you, ma'am?
Guest	You can contact me by calling 562-465-8966. It's my mobile number.
Elena	How are you paying?
Guest	I'll pay by Master Card when I check out.
Elena	Your room has been reserved from October 22nd to 24th and your reservation number is SJ2225. Thank you for calling and we are looking forward to your visit.
Guest	Thank you. Good bye.

Conversation 4 Confirming Reservations

"Let me check your reservation details."

Reservation This is the reservation desk. May I help you?

Guest Yes, I'd like to confirm my reservation. Can you help me with that?

Reservation Absolutely, sir. Would you tell me your name and reservation number?

Guest My name is Robert Taylor, but I am wondering I don't remember my reservation number.

Reservation No problem. Let me check your reservation details. You reserved a twin room for 2 nights from March 7th to March 9th. You requested a mountain view and a nonsmoking room.

Guest That's right. Can you send me a confirmation e-mail?

Reservation Certainly, sir. May I have your e-mail address?

Guest My e-mail address is robert4727@gmail.com.

Reservation Yes, sir. I'll send it to you right away.

Guest Thank you so much.

Reservation You're welcome, sir

Conversation 5 Dealing with Guests' Problems

"I can offer you our walk-up rate"

Front Desk	Good afternoon, sir. What can I do for you?
Guest	Hi. I need a room for this evening.
Front Desk	Do you have a reservation?
Guest	No, I don't. My flight's been delayed until tomorrow evening and I need to stay in the city overnight.
Front Desk	I can offer you our walk-up rate which is $280 per night for a double room including breakfast.
Guest	That's a lot more expensive than I expected. Is that the cheapest rate you have?
Front Desk	I'm afraid so. We're very busy tonight.
Guest	Ok. I'll take it.
Front Desk	Fine. Could you fill in this guest registration card for me, please?
Guest	Ok. What time do I have to check out tomorrow?
Front Desk	Our usual check-out time is 11 o'clock, sir, but, with this rate you can have a late check-out until 2 p.m.
Guest	That's great. Thank you very much.

Conversation 6 Cancelling Reservations

"I'm sorry, but I'd like to cancel my reservation for the hotel."

Colin Good morning. Peninsula Hotel, Colin speaking.

Guest I'm sorry, but I'd like to cancel my reservation for the hotel.

Colin May I have your name and reservation number?

Guest It's Ms. Yang and my reservation number is MH374ET.

Colin Ok, Ms. Yang, I've cancelled your reservation for you. There's no cancellation charge because you've cancelled within our 48-hour cancellation deadline.

Guest That's good. Thank you.

Colin Would you like me to send you a confirmation e-mail?

Guest Yes, please. Thanks for the help.

Colin We hope to serve you next time.

3. More Tips For You

Hotel Room Types

Room Types	Description
 [Single Room]	1인용 객실 또는 싱글베드가 있는 1인실을 의미합니다. 싱글룸의 기준 면적은 $13m^2$ 이상이어야 하며 침대의 표준규격은 길이 195cm × 넓이 90cm 이상, 담요규격은 길이 230cm × 넓이 170cm 이상이어야 합니다.
 [Double Room]	더블베드를 갖추고 있는 2인용 객실을 의미합니다. 더블베드 크기에 따라 킹사이즈 / 퀸사이즈로 다시 세분화되기도 합니다. 객실의 넓이는 $16m^2$ 이상이며 침대의 폭은 보통 싱글베드의 1.5배로 표준규격이 길이 195cm × 넓이 138cm 이상이고, 담요규격은 길이 230cm × 넓이 200cm 이상이어야 합니다.

 [Twin Room]	싱글베드 또는 세미더블베드 2개가 포함되어 있는 2인용 객실입니다.
 [Triple Room]	싱글베드 3개 혹은 더블베드 1개에 엑스트라 베드 1개가 포함된 3인용 객실로서 주로 가족 단위 투숙객이 이용합니다.
 [Suite Room]	면적이 $26m^2$ 이상의 객실로서, 욕실이 딸린 침실 1개와 거실 겸 응접실 1개 총 2실로 짜인 객실을 의미합니다. 호텔에 따라 침실이 2개 이상 있기도 하고 거실과 응접실이 따로따로 분리되어 있는 경우도 있습니다.

4. DIY

How do you say the following sentences in English?

(1) 4월 5일에 2박 조식 포함된 객실을 예약하고 싶습니다.

→

(2) 죄송하지만 이번 주에는 객실이 만실입니다.

→

(3) 예약사항을 팩스로 보내주시겠습니까?

→

(4) 안타깝게도 여행 일정이 취소되어 예약을 취소하고 싶습니다.

→

(5) 바다 전망 대신 산 전망 객실은 이용 가능합니다.

→

A Story Behind the Hotel Brand

Hilton Hotel "Be My Guest"

힐튼 호텔의 창업자 Conrad N. Hilton은 노르웨이계 독일인 이민자의 아들로 태어나 가난한 어린 시절을 보냅니다. 힐튼은 고향을 떠나 텍사스로 와서 호텔 청소부로 일을 시작하게 되고, 1919년 미국 텍사스주 시스코의 작은 호텔이었던 <The Mobley>를 인수하면서 힐튼 호텔의 역사가 시작됩니다. 1925년 제1호 힐튼 호텔을 개장하지만 아직 에어컨이 발명되기 전이었기 때문에 엘리베이터, 세탁물 활송 장치, 환기구 등 고객이 사용하지 않는 설비를 건물 서쪽에 배치하여 객실에 서쪽의 햇살이 들지 않도록 설계하였습니다. 경제공황으로 1931년 큰 위기를 맞기도 하지만 미국 최고의 호텔을 만들겠다는 그의 꿈과 신념은 전 세계로 뻗어나가게 되고 현재 103개 국가 및 영토에 5,100여개 약 838,000개의 객실을 보유한 가장 성공한 호텔 기업으로 자리 잡으며 힐튼이라는 브랜드는 호텔의 대명사가 됩니다. 힐튼 호텔의 성공비결을 묻는 이들에게 콘래드 힐튼은 다음과 같이 대답합니다.

"이 철근막대기는 5달러 정도 됩니다. 이것을 불에 달군 다음 망치로 두드려 말발굽을 만들면 10달러 50센트 정도를 받을 수 있습니다. 이를 바늘로 만들면 67배, 면도날을 만들면 657배, 스위스 명품 시계에 들어가는 밸런스 스프링을 만들면 그 가치가 5만 배 상승합니다. <나>라는 원자재를 어떻게 이용하는가가 성공의 관건입니다."

"성공은 행동과 관련이 있습니다. 성공하는 사람은 계속해서 움직이고 또 움직입니다. 물론 그들도 가끔씩 실수를 하지만 움직이기를 절대 중단하는 법이 없습니다."

이처럼 텍사스의 작은 호텔에서 자신의 꿈을 실현시키고 더 큰 꿈을 꾸며 평생을 노력해온 그의 노력과 신념은 많은 호텔리어에게 교훈으로 남고 있습니다.

[Conrad Nicholson Hilton]

[콘래드 힐튼이 1919년 매입한 텍사스 시스코에 있는 모블리 호텔]

Unit 2

Checking-in

We will learn
- how to explain about check-in
- how to make polite suggestions
- how to find a solution for a guest

Hotel English

1. What They Do

체크인은 프론트데스크(Front Desk)의 주요 업무 중 하나로, 예약한 고객이 프론트데스크에 도착하면 예약사항(예약번호, 성명, 연락처, 객실형태 등)을 확인하고 등록 절차를 거쳐 객실을 배정하게 됩니다. 객실을 배정할 때에는 고객의 요청사항 혹은 선호하는 부분을 우선시하며 재방문 고객의 경우에는 고객의 호텔 이용 히스토리를 사전에 파악한 후 재방문에 대한 감사인사를 전하는 것도 잊지 말아야 합니다.

체크인 과정

① (인사) 안녕하십니까? 무엇을 도와드릴까요?
② (예약확인) 예약자분 성함이나 예약 번호를 알 수 있을까요?
③ (모니터확인) 네 고객님, 디럭스룸으로 2박 예약하셨습니다.
④ (등록카드) 고객이 등록카드에 주소, 여권번호, 연락처 등을 기입한 후 서명을 받는다.
⑤ (객실키) 고객이 등록카드를 작성하는 동안 객실키를 준비한다.
⑥ (예치금결제) 예약자 이름과 신용카드 이름을 확인 후 예치금(보증금)을 결제한다.
⑦ (출력) 체크아웃시 환불(결제취소) 됨을 안내한 뒤 카드전표를 출력하여 전달한다.
⑧ (키전달) 고객에게 객실번호를 안내한 후 벨맨을 소개한다.
⑨ (인사) 감사합니다. 편안한 시간 보내시기 바랍니다.

2. Conversations

Conversation 1 Checking in Guests

"Do you have a reservation?"

Front Desk	Good afternoon, sir. Do you have a reservation?
Guest	Yes, I do. My name is James Brown.
Front Desk	One moment, sir. Let me check the list. You're staying with us for 3 nights.
Guest	Yes, that's correct.
Front Desk	How many are there in your party?
Guest	We're a family of four. I'm traveling with my wife and 2 children.
Front Desk	Do you prefer connecting rooms or a triple room with an extra bed?
Guest	A triple room with an extra bed will be fine.
Front Desk	Excellent. How will you be paying, sir?
Guest	With Visa card.
Front Desk	Ok, thank you. Here's your key card for your room and vouchers for breakfast. The buffet restaurant for breakfast opens from 6 to 11 in the morning. It's on the 3rd floor.
Guest	Thank you very much for your kindness.
Front Desk	My pleasure, sir.

Conversation 2 Confirming Reservation Details

"Please fill out this registration card and sign here."

Front Desk	Welcome to the Ritz Carlton. May I help you?
Guest	I have a reservation. My name is Paul Smith.
Front Desk	Just a moment, please. Let me check your reservation. You booked a deluxe room for 2 nights, so you are checking out on Friday, right?
Guest	That's right. Non-smoking, too.
Front Desk	Did you request a nonsmoking room facing the ocean?
Guest	Yes, I did. Do you have a room on the ground floor? I have a acrophobia.
Front Desk	Certainly, sir. We have a room available on the ground floor. May I have your passport, please?
Guest	Sure. Here it is.
Front Desk	Please fill out this registration card and sign here.
Guest	All right. Here you go.
Front Desk	How will you be paying for the room?
Guest	With American Express card.
Front Desk	I'm very sorry sir, we don't accept American Express card. Do you have another card?
Guest	Then I will pay in cash.
Front Desk	Thank you. Here is your room key and your room number is 101. The bellman will show you to your room. Enjoy your stay with us.
Guest	Thank you.

Conversation 3 Apologizing for Mistakes

"I do apologize. There must be something wrong in our computer system."

Guest Good morning. I'd like to check in now.
I made a reservation on your web site.

Front Desk Under what name is your reservation, sir?

Guest It's under my name, Jay Chung.

Front Desk Just a minute, sir. Let me find your name on the computer.

Guest I made my reservation a week ago.

Front Desk How do you spell your last name?

Guest C-H-U-N-G

Front Desk I'm very sorry, but your name is not listed.
There must be some errors.

Guest I have my confirmation e-mail right here.

Front Desk Let me take a look at that, please.

Guest Sure. Here you are.

Front Desk Oh, sorry. I do apologize. There must be something wrong in our computer system.
I'll get you a room right away.

Conversation 4 Early Check-in

"I'm sorry. Your room isn't quite ready yet."

Front Desk Good morning, ma'am. How are you today?

Guest Good, thank you. I have a reservation in the name of Portman.

Front Desk Ms. Natalie Portman?

Guest That's right.

Front Desk I'm sorry, Ms. Portman. Your room isn't quite ready yet. Normally our check-in is from 2 p.m.

Guest I already checked your hotel's check-in time but my flight arrived early.

Front Desk I totally understand but Housekeeping are still cleaning the room.

Guest That's not good. What do you suggest I do?

Front Desk May I suggest you have a cup of coffee in the bar? When your room is ready, I'll come and get you.
Is that alright?

Guest Ok, but how long will that be?

Front Desk I will ask Housekeeping to do your room as quickly as possible.

Guest I'd appreciate it. How do I get to the bar?

Front Desk Just go around the corner to your right, sir.

Conversation 5 Check-in for Walk-in Guest

"Do you have any rooms available for tonight?"

Front Desk	Good afternoon, ma'am. What can I do for you?
Guest	Do you have any rooms available for tonight?
Front Desk	Did you make a reservation for your room?
Guest	No, I don't have a reservation.
Front Desk	How long will you be staying, ma'am?
Guest	Two nights.
Front Desk	What type of room do you want?
Guest	A single room on a high floor.
Front Desk	I will check the room for you. Fortunately, we can offer you that room.
Guest	How much does it cost per night?
Front Desk	It costs $180 per night plus tax and service charge, ma'am. Would that be acceptable?
Guest	That sounds fine. I'll take it. Thank you for helping me.

Conversation 6 Taking Reservation Details

"Let me check your reservation."

Guest	Good morning. Can I check in now? My name is Peter Williams. I made a reservation through an online travel agency.
Front Desk	Wait for a minute, please. Let me check your reservation. How do you spell your last name?
Guest	W-I-L-L-I-A-M-S
Front Desk	OK. We have your reservation. May I have your business card for registration?
Guest	No, I don't have one with me.
Front Desk	Then, could you fill out this registration form, sir?
Guest	Sure. Can I pay the room rate by traveler's check?
Front Desk	I'm afraid not. Cash or Credit Card only, I'm afraid. It is hotel policy.
Guest	Ok, then I will pay by credit card.
Front Desk	May I have your credit card to make an imprint, while you are filling out the registration form?
Guest	Here you go.
Front Desk	Thank you, Mr. Williams. Here's your room key. You can take the elevator on your left.
Guest	Thank you very much.
Front Desk	Enjoy your stay with us.

3. More Tips For You

Connecting Room vs. Adjoining Room

Connecting Room

객실 내에 connecting door가 있어서 복도를 통하지 않고 이 connecting door를 이용하여 옆방과 연결하여 한 객실처럼 이용 가능한 객실을 의미합니다. connecting room은 보통 가족 단위의 투숙객들이 이용하기 편리합니다.

[Connecting Room]

Adjoining Room

나란히 인접해있는 객실을 의미하는 것으로 객실과 객실 사이에 내부 연결문이 따로 없으므로 복도를 통해서만 출입이 가능한 형태입니다.

예를 들어, 1101호 객실과 1102호 객실은 adjoining room이며 만약 1101호 객실과 1102호 객실 내부에 연결문이 있다면 connecting room이 되는 것입니다.

[Adjoining Room]

4. DIY

Make the sentences with the given words below.

(1) 체크인하고 싶습니다. 호텔 웹사이트를 통해 예약했습니다.

→

(2) 예약이 확인되지 않고 있습니다. 예약 번호 좀 알 수 있을까요?

→

(3) 저희 체크인 시간은 오후 3시라서 조금 기다리셔야 합니다.

→

(4) 결제는 어떻게 하시겠습니까?

→

(5) 고객등록카드 작성 부탁드리겠습니다.

→

A Story Behind the Hotel Brand

Four Seasons Hotels & Resorts
"샤워기 수압부터 크루아상 굽기까지 똑같이"

포시즌스호텔앤리조트(Four Seasons Hotel & Resort)는 1961년 캐나다 토론토의 작은 모터호텔에서 시작하여 현재 43개국에 102개의 호텔과 리조트를 운영하고 있습니다. '현대사회의 여행자를 위한 사치'를 모토로 최고 수준의 서비스를 강조하는 포시즌스는 1970년대 '최고급 중소 규모 호텔 개발'을 목표로 삼았습니다. 당시 대부분의 호텔들은 서비스와 시설의 질이 서로 달랐지만 포시즌스는 최고급이면서도 일정한 서비스를 제공하기 위하여 많은 노력을 기울입니다. 모든 포시즌스는 샤워기의 수압부터 크루아상의 굽기까지 일정할 정도로 서비스 및 시설의 표준화 방식을 까다롭게 지켜내고 있습니다.

포시즌스의 세심한 서비스에 대한 고집을 엿볼 수 있는 유명한 일화 하나가 있습니다. 포시즌스 호텔 레스토랑에서 조식을 즐기던 미국인 부부 두 커플이 호텔 서비스에 대하여 이야기를 나누고 있었습니다. 그 중 한 명이 "이 호텔은 모든 면에서 더할 나위 없이 좋은데 딱 한 가지가 불만족스러워. 방에 있는 4개의 베개 중 2개는 깃털 베개, 나머지 2개는 메모리폼 베개인데 나는 4개 모두 깃털베개였으면 좋겠단 말이지" 같은 날 밤 침대로 가보니 이 남자의 방 베개는 4개 모두 깃털베개로 바뀌어 있었습니다. 남자는 베개에 대하여 공식적으로 불만을 제기한 적도 없었고, 베개를 바꿔달라는 요청을 하지도 않았는데 어찌된 영문일까요? 알고 보니 식사 중에 이들의 대화를 듣게 된 직원이 매니저에게 다시 이 매니저가 하우스키퍼에서 관련 내용을 전달하고 베개를 교체해준 것이었습니다.

포시즌스의 아시아 지역 부사장 크리스토퍼 노튼이 한 인터뷰에 언급했던 것처럼 포시즌스는 쿠키를 자르듯 개성 없는 호텔과 리조트가 되려고 하지 않으며 최고급의 표준화된 서비스를 제공하되 각기 다른 개성과 매력으로 소비자들에게 꾸준히 사랑받고 있습니다.

뿐만 아니라 2017년부터 <포시즌스 프라이빗 제트>라는 호텔형 여객기를 선보였습니다. <포시즌스 프라이빗 제트>는 보잉 757기를 총 52석의 프리미엄 좌석으로 개조한 호텔 전용기로 약 3주간 여행하면서 세계 전역의 포시즌스 호텔에 투숙하는 역대 최고급 일정의 세계 일주 투어 패키지입니다.

세계 일주 투어 패키지는 유럽과 아시아 지역의 독특하고 개성 있는 지역 음식을 체험할 수 있는 <컬리너리 디스커버리>, 세계 각국의 레저 활동을 즐길 수 있는 <글로벌 게이트웨이>, 8개국의 다양한 문화를 탐방하는 <인터내셔널 인트리그> 등의 3가지 프로그램들로 구성됩니다.

[포시즌스 프라이빗 제트기]

[포시즌스 프라이빗 제트기 내부]

Unit 03

Door Desk

We will learn
- how to guide guests to the reception
- how to organize transport
- how to handle guests' belongings

Hotel English

1. What They Do

Doorman

고객이 정문에 도착하면 가장 먼저 마주하는 직원이므로 호텔의 첫인상을 전달하는 중요한 역할이기도 합니다. 도어맨은 고객을 맞이하기 위하여 현관문의 2m-3m 전방에서 차량이 정차할 수 있는 위치를 수신호로 안내하고 차량이 정차하면 왼손으로 문을 열고 오른손은 고객의 머리를 보호하며 정중한 인사와 함께 고객의 하차를 돕습니다. 고객이 차량에서 내리면 차량의 문을 닫고 신속하게 고객의 수하물을 받아 운반을 도운 뒤, 벨맨에게 수하물 개수와 특이사항 등을 인계합니다.

도어맨의 업무는 계절이나 시간과 관계없이 항상 외부에서 이루어진다는 특징이 있으며 고객이 가장 첫 번째로 만나는 호텔 직원이기 때문에 다양한 문의가 수시로 발생하는 부서이기도 합니다. 따라서 도어맨은 당일 예정된 호텔 내부 행사 정보 뿐 아니라 호텔 이용에 필요한 각종 정보에서부터 주변 관광지에 대한 정보에 이르기까지 다양하고 구체적인 내용들을 숙지하고 있어야 합니다.
도어맨의 주요 업무는 다음과 같습니다.

- 고객영접 및 환송서비스
- 호텔 출입문 개폐관리
- 정보제공 및 안내서비스
- 차량안내 및 교통정리
- 차량호출 및 수배업무
- 주차대행서비스
- 호텔출입통제업무

2. Conversations

Conversation 1 Checking Guests' Baggages

"Do you have any bags that I can help you with?"

Doorman	Good afternoon. Do you have any bags that I can help you with?
Guest	Yes, I have three bags in the trunk.
Doorman	I'll pick them out, ma'am. Our bellman will take care of your baggage afterward.
Guest	That's good. Where can I check in?
Doorman	The reception desk is over there in the center. Please watch out for the revolving door.
Guest	Thank you.
Doorman	It's my pleasure. Enjoy your stay with us!

Conversation 2 Offering to Help

"May I help you with your luggage?"

Doorman Good morning, sir. May I help you with your luggage?

Guest Thanks a lot. Please take care of my luggage.

Doorman Certainly, sir. Just leave them here and step this way over to the front desk.

Guest Thank you.

Conversation 3 Saying Farewell to a Guest

"Did you enjoy your stay with us?"

Doorman Good afternoon, sir. Are you leaving now?

Guest Yes, I am.

Doorman Did you enjoy your stay with us?

Guest Sure. I had a wonderful time.

Doorman Do you need a taxi?

Guest Yes, please. I'm straight going to the airport.

Doorman Would you like to wait in the lobby, sir?
I will let you know when a taxi arrives.

Guest Thanks. How long does it take to get there from here?

Doorman Normally about an hour, but it depends on traffic.

Conversation 4 Giving Information to Guests

"We have a valet parking service."

Doorman Good evening, madam. Welcome to Peninsula Hotel.
Can I help you with your suitcase?

Guest No, thanks. It's not heavy so I can carry it by myself.
Where should I park my car?

Doorman We have a valet parking service. Just leave your car here.
I will take care of everything.

Guest That's great. Thank you.

Doorman You're welcome. Enjoy your stay, madam.

Conversation 5 Organizing Transport

"Could you please book an airport limousine for me?"

Doorman Good morning, sir. What can I do for you?

Guest Could you please book an airport limousine for me?

Doorman Sure. Can I have your flight schedule?

Guest My flight is scheduled for 3 p.m. from Incheon.

Doorman Since international flight passengers must be checked in at least 2 hours in advance, I will reserve a limousine at 1 o'clock.

Guest Thank you.

Conversation 6 Bringing a Car for Guests

"Ok, I'll bring your car immediately."

Doorman How may I help you?

Guest Could you get my car, please?

Doorman Of course. What is your vehicle number?

Guest The number is 2346. It is a white SUV.

Doorman Ok, I'll bring your car immediately.

Guest Thanks a lot.

Doorman It's my pleasure.

3. More Tips For You

사라져가고 있는 Key - 호텔 객실 도어시스템의 진화

과거 호텔 객실 키들은 사진에서처럼 무거운 쇠로 만들어진 열쇠가 일반적이었습니다. 물론 지금도 유럽의 수많은 호텔들은 금속 열쇠를 고수하고 있는 곳이 많으며, 일부 현대적인 호텔들은 열쇠가 주는 특유의 고풍스러움을 표현하고자 옛날 방식의 금속 열쇠를 사용하기도 합니다. 시간이 흐르면서 호텔 투숙객들이 조금 더 안전하고 편리하게 머무를 수 있도록 키카드 방식이 도입되었고, 키카드는 출입 기능 뿐 아니라 호텔의 이미지를 담아내는 하나의 표현수단이기도 합니다. 호텔 객실 도어시스템은 끊임없이 진화하고 있으며, 최근에는 대형 체인 호텔들을 중심으로 keyless system을 도입 혹은 검토 중에 있습니다.

힐튼은 이미 미국과 캐나다의 약 1,700여 계열 호텔에서 스마트폰 어플리케이션을 방의 열쇠로 대신 사용하는 시스템을 도입하고 있습니다. 2018년 말까지 세계 5,000여개의 계열 호텔의 절반에 도입하는 것을 목표로 적극적으로 움직이고 있습니다. 우리나라에서는 2017년 1월 SK네트웍스 워커힐이 인천공항 이용객들을 위하여 오픈한 캡슐호텔 <다락 휴>에서 keyless system을 도입하여 예약 및 체크인·체크아웃, 조명 및 온도 조절까지 모든 과정을 스마트폰으로 손쉽고 빠르게 이용할 수 있도록 운영 중에 있습니다.

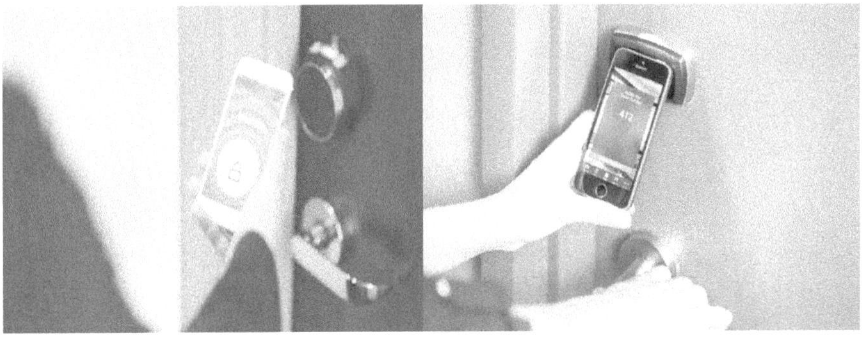

4. DIY

Practice Role-Playing with your partner

[Situation 1 : Welcoming guests and finding out what guests need]

Doorman :

Guest :

Doorman :

Guest :

Doorman :

Guest :

Doorman :

Guest :

[Situation 2 : Escorting guests to the reception desk and helping them with their luggages.]

Doorman :

Guest :

Doorman :

Guest :

Doorman :

Guest :

Doorman :

Guest :

A Story Behind the Hotel Brand

The Ritz-Carlton Hotel

"리츠가 가는 곳이라면 나도 간다."

1850년에 스위스의 니더발트(Niederwald) 촌장의 열세번째 아들로 태어난 세자르 리츠(Cesar Ritz)는 열다섯살에 스위스 브리그의 호텔에서 웨이터로 일한 것을 시작으로 1878년에 루체른에 있는 그랜드 호텔의 매니저가 되었고, 1888년에 요리사 오귀스트 에스코피에(Auguste Escoffier)와 함께 바덴-바덴(Baden-Baden)에 레스토랑을 열었습니다. 1889년부터 1897년까지는 영국 런던 사보이 호텔의 매니저로 일하는 등 호텔업계에서 두각을 나타내기 시작한 그는 세심한 서비스 제공과 열정으로 왕족과 명사들의 신뢰를 얻기 시작하였고 그가 호텔을 옮겨 다닐 때마다 그의 단골 고객들은 그를 따라다니며 "리츠가 가는 곳이라면 나도 간다"라는 말이 나올 정도로 찬사를 받게 됩니다.

유럽 사교계에서 무한한 신뢰와 사랑을 받았을 뿐 아니라 당시로서는 획기적인 다양한 아이디어를 내놓기도 합니다. 한 예로, 당시 상류층은 외출하는 일이 거의 없었는데 상류층 여성들을 위하여 레스토랑에 오케스트라를 도입하여 식사와 문화생활을 동시에 즐길 수 있도록 하거나 오페라 감상 후 식사로 이어질 수 있게끔 서퍼(supper: 격식을 갖춘 정식만찬)를 제공하여 레스토랑 영업시간 관련 법률까지 바꿔놓기도 합니다. 이후에 일류호텔들을 경영하며 정상에 오르게 되고, 1989년 파리 방돔 광장에 리츠파리(Ritz Paris)를 오픈합니다. 이 호텔은 전기조명과 전화기를 설치한 최초의 호텔이기도 하며 전등갓 커버, 욕실 커튼, 욕실용품 등을 사람이 아름다워 보이는 복숭아 색깔로 통일하는 등 세심한 차별화 전략으로 새로운 호텔 역사를 만들어 갑니다.

1918년 10월 26일, 세자르 리츠는 세상을 떠났지만 고급이 아닌 일류를 목표로 삼으며 현대 호스피탈리티 서비스의 한 획을 그은 그는 지금까지도 수많은 호텔리어들에게 존중받는 진정한 "왕들의 호텔리어, 호텔리어의 왕"으로 불리고 있습니다.
세자르 리츠의 경영 철학을 계승하여 최고급 시설과 호스피탈리티 정신으로 세계 최상류층 고객들을 보유한 리츠칼튼 호텔에는 모든 직원이 반드시 지니고 있는 카드가 있습니다. 크레도(Credo : 신조)라는 이 카드에는 다음과 같은 문구가 새겨져 있습니다.

We are Ladies and Gentlemen serving Ladies and Gentlemen
우리는 신사숙녀를 섬기는 신사숙녀입니다.

일류 호텔 브랜드답게 직원 모두 신사숙녀라는 수식어에 걸 맞는 품격 있는 서비스를 제공하는 것이야말로 일류 고객을 맞이할 기본자세라고 할 수 있습니다.

[César Ritz, 1850년 2월 23일 - 1918년 10월 26일]

[Hôtel Ritz Paris]

[Hôtel Ritz Paris Vendôme Suite Room]

Unit 04

Bell Desk

We will learn
- how to take a guest to his or her room
- how to deal with guest's luggage
- how to handle complaints

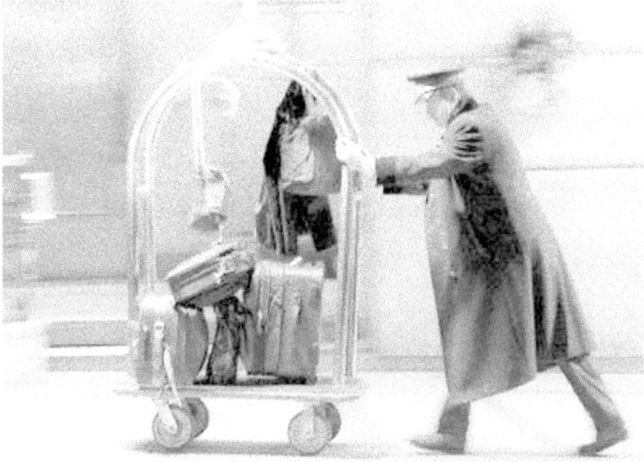

Hotel English

1. What They Do

Bellman

고객이 호텔 정문에서 도어맨의 안내를 받아 로비에 들어서면 두 번째로 벨맨의 영접을 받게 됩니다. 벨맨의 기본 업무는 고객을 객실까지 안내, 고객의 짐을 전달·수거·보관 하는 것이며 호텔 시설 안내, 로비관리, 각종 메시지 전달, paging service, 객실 변경, 차량 수배 등의 업무를 수행합니다. 벨맨은 당일 객실 판매현황과 각종 행사 진행 현황을 숙지하고 로비 내 지정된 위치에서 밝은 표정으로 양발을 30cm 정도 벌리고 두 손은 벨트부분에 포개어 허리를 편 바른 자세로 대기합니다.

벨맨이 안내해야할 객실 내 정보

- 객실키 사용법
- TV 이용 안내 및 유료 채널 안내
- 비상구 위치 및 비상용품 사용방법
- 냉난방 작동법 및 온도조절방법
- 전화사용법
- 미니바 이용 안내
- 개인금고 사용법

2. Conversations

Conversation 1 Escorting a Guest

"Let me escort you to your room, sir."

Bellman Are these all your bags?
Guest Yes, these are all mine.
Bellman Let me escort you to your room, sir.
Please come with me.
Take the elevator, please. May I have your key card?
Guest Here it is.
Bellman Thank you.
When you go up to your room, you should insert this key card here before you press the button of the floor.
But when you go down anywhere, you don't need to.
Your room is on the 12th floor.
Guest Thank you very much.

(getting out of the elevator)

Bellman Your room is on the left side. This way, please.

(arriving at the door)

Bellman This is your room. Please go in. Do you like the room?
Guest Much better and more spacious than I expected.
Bellman I'm glad you like it, sir.

Conversation 2 Showing a Room

"If you need any other help, please call the bell desk at any time."

Bellman Here is your room, ma'am.

Guest Good. Put the bags there, please. By the way, it's very cold in here. How can I turn the air conditioning down?

Bellman The temperature controller is right here on the wall.
Let me tell you more details about the room.
Here is the light switch for the bathroom.
Here's the remote control beside the TV set.
We have local channels and cable TV.
The mini bar is in the refrigerator over there.
Only two bottles of water are complimentary.
You'll get charged for what you eat when you check out.

Guest Oh, I see. Thank you very much. This is for you.

Bellman I'm sorry, ma'am. Our hotel has no-tipping policy.

Guest Really? Thank you anyway.

Bellman You're welcome, ma'am. Enjoy your stay.
If you need any other help, please call the bell desk at any time.

Conversation 3 Helping a Guest with Baggages

"Let me send someone up to your room soon."

Bellman	Good evening. This is the bell desk. How may I help you?
Guest	This room is 1612. Can you send me a bellman? I'm checking out in 20 minutes.
Bellman	Yes, sir. How many bags do you have?
Guest	I have two suitcases and one carry-on bag.
Bellman	I see. Let me send someone up to your room soon.

Conversation 4 Holding a Baggage

"Let me keep your luggage until you come back."

Guest Hi. Can I leave my bags at the hotel?
I just checked out, but I'd like to go shopping before leaving for the airport.

Bellman Sure. Let me keep your luggage until you come back.
Can I have your name and room number?

Guest My name is Kelly David, and my room number was 1008.

Bellman OK. Here is your luggage claim tag. Please show me the tag when you pick up your bags.
Have a nice time.

Conversation 5 Ordering a Taxi

"I'm going to call your room when your taxi arrives."

Bellman	May I help you?
Guest	Yes. Can you order me a taxi for later today, please?
Bellman	Of course, sir. What time do you need it?
Guest	I have to be at the Convention Center at 9 a.m.
Bellman	Ok. I'll order you a taxi for a quarter to 9. What's your room number, sir?
Guest	I'm in room 1002.
Bellman	Ok. I'm going to call your room when your taxi arrives.
Guest	Thank you very much.
Bellman	You're welcome. Have a nice day.

Conversation 6 Handling Complaints

"I'm very sorry for the inconvenience."

Bellman Good morning. How may I assist you?

Guest I'm Samantha Wilson in room 317. I've been waiting for my bags to be sent up for almost 30 minutes!

Bellman I'm terribly sorry for the delay, Ms. Wilson. Do you have a baggage tag number?

Guest Yes, it's 1102.

Bellman I'll check on that right away and get back to you, ma'am.

(A few minutes later)

Bellman Hello, Ms. Wilson. This is Peter from Bell Desk. Your bags are on the way now. I'm very sorry for the inconvenience.

3. More Tips For You

British vs. American Vocabulary

같은 언어일지라도 영국식 영어와 미국식 영어는 시제나 동사, 전치사 사용 등 문법에서 약간의 차이를 보이며 발음, 철자, 어휘 등에서 다른 점들이 있습니다. 다양한 배경과 문화를 지니고 다양한 언어를 구사하는 서로 다른 계층들이 우리의 고객이므로 전문적인 호텔리어가 되기 위해서는 각각의 차이와 표현법들을 정확하게 이해하는 것이 필요합니다.

British	American	Meaning
anti-clockwise	counter-clockwise	
bill	bill, check	
block of flats	apartment building	
car park	parking lot	
chemist's shop	drugstore, pharmacy	
chips	fries, French fries	
diversion	detour	
drink-driving	drunk driving	
driving licence	driver's license	
dustbin	garbage can, trash can	
estate agent	real estate agent	
flat	apartment, flat, studio	
ground floor	first floor	
high street	main street	
holiday	vacation	
lift	elevator	
motorbike	motorcycle	
pavement	sidewalk	
postcode	zip code	
timetable	schedule	
tin	can	
underground, tube	subway	

4. DIY

You work at the bell desk. You are calling to one of your guests and telling her the taxi has arrived. Put the sentences into the correct order. The first sentence has done for you.

1	Guest	Hello? This is Anna White from room 709.
( )	Guest	Good morning
( )	You	That sounds perfect, madam. I'll tell the taxi driver that you'll be here soon.
( )	You	Good morning, Mrs White. This is Benjamin from Bell Desk.
( )	Guest	Please tell the driver I'll be down in 10 minutes.
( )	You	I'm calling to let you know that your taxi has arrived.
( )	Guest	Thank you Benjamin.

1	Guest	Can I leave my bags for a moment after checking out?
( )	You	Ok, Ms. Eileen. I will put your bags over here
( )	You	Of course you can, sir. May I ask you name and room number?
( )	You	You're welcome Please keep your baggage tag
( )	Guest	I'm Eileen and I was in room 2786
( )	Guest	I appreciate it

A Story Behind the Hotel Brand

Banyan Tree Hotels & Resorts
"바니안 나무에서 시작된 반얀트리의 역사"

1984년 11월 아내와 함께 태국 푸껫 방타오만 해변을 거닐던 30대 싱가포르 출신 사업가 호권핑(何光平)은 암초로 둘러싸인 지형을 발견합니다. 바닷물은 새파랗고 주변에 제대로 된 나무 한 그루도 없이 특유의 이국적인 분위기를 자아내던 그곳을 매입하게 되고 푸켓에도 하와이 같은 리조트를 짓고자 결심하게 됩니다. 하지만 그 부지는 주석 탄광 개발로 심하게 오염되어 유엔개발계획(UNDP)이 '회복 불가능한 땅'으로 분류한 곳이었습니다. 물이 유난히 파란 것도 탄광에서 흘러나온 산성 성분 때문이라는 것을 알게 됩니다. 그러나 호권핑과 클레어창 부부는 포기하지 않고 7000여 그루의 나무를 심고 바닷물 정화에 적극적으로 나서면서 '삶의 질'에 대하여 끊임없이 고민합니다. 그리고 1994년 마침내 부부는 태국 푸켓에 자연주의를 표방한 <Banyan Tree Resort>를 개관합니다. 인도인들 사이에 새 생명, 쉼터를 주는 나무, 장수와 자손 번성의 상징 등 신성하게 여겨지는 반얀 나무(바이안 나무)에서 그 이름을 따서 아시아 최초의 스파 리조트가 탄생하게 됩니다.

당시 일대 아시안 리조트 붐이 일었던 시기였기만 '휴식'을 주제로 한 스파리조트는 드물었기에 반얀트리의 등장은 신선한 충격이었습니다. 태국식 바닥재의 스파 룸과 천정 없는 프라이빗한 커플용 스파 빌라에서 천연 재료를 사용하는 스파 프로그램을 운영하며 '최고의 스파'로 자리 잡고 아시아식 스파 문화를 전 세계에 전파하는 역할을 하게 됩니다.

반얀트리는 GIF(Green Imperative Fund)라는 기금을 설치하여 고객으로부터 1박에 약 2달러 가량의 돈을 모금하고 이 기금으로 리조트가 있는 지역의 자연 보호 및 계몽 활동에 사용합니다. 한 예로 몰디브의 반얀트리 바빈파루(Banyan Tree

Vabbinfaru)에서는 멸종 위기에 놓인 바다거북을 보호하고 엘리뇨 현상으로 백화된 산호를 재생하는 프로그램을 운영하는 등 이처럼 반얀트리는 자연과 인간이 공존할 수 있는 지속가능한 발전의 가치와 의미를 전달해주고 있습니다.

[Banyan Tree Logo]

[Green Imperative Fund Banyan Tree]

[Banyan Tree Bali]

[Banyan Tree Bangkok]

Unit 05

Telephone Service

We will learn
- how to transfer a call to a guest's room
- how to deal with guest's request
- how to make information clear

Hotel English

1. What They Do

전화업무는 고객과 직접 대면은 아니지만 직원의 목소리와 태도, 신속한 처리 방식 등에 따라 호텔에 대한 이미지나 만족도가 결정되는 중요한 부분이기도 합니다. 전화교환실은 호텔 대표번호로 걸려오는 전화를 관련부서로 연결하고 고객들의 시외전화, 국제전화, 모닝콜 업무 등을 담당하는 부서입니다. 전화교환실의 직원은 오퍼레이터(operator)라고 불리며 최근에는 오퍼레이터를 거치지 않고 직접 외부로 전화를 걸 수 있도록 하는 호텔이 늘어나고 있는 추세이며, 자동화시스템으로 해당 부서로 자동 연결되거나 자동 모닝콜 같은 기능을 도입하고 있습니다.

전화교환실 오퍼레이터의 주요업무를 요약해보면 다음과 같습니다.

- 국제 전화 및 연결 업무
- 모닝콜 업무
- 귀빈객실의 체크 업무
- 프론트에서 단체명단을 받아 모닝콜 및 식사 시간, 장소, 메뉴 등을 안내
- 기타 비상상황을 당직지배인에게 보고

2. Conversations

Conversation 1 Wake-up Call

"Could you give me a wake-up call at 7:00 tomorrow morning, please?"

Morgan Good evening, Intercontinental Hotel. Morgan speaking.

Guest This is Matthew Arnold in room 1320. Could you give me a wake-up call at 7:00 tomorrow morning, please?

Morgan Certainly, Mr. Arnold. Your wake-up call has just been registered.

Guest Thank you. Good night.

Morgan Good night, sir.

(next morning)

Guest Hello?

Morgan Good morning, Mr. Arnold. This is your 7 a.m. wake-up call.

Guest Thank you.

Morgan You're welcome, sir. Have a great day.

Conversation 2 Taking a Message

"Can I take a message for you?"

Reception Good morning, Palace Hotel. How can I help you?

Guest Hello. Can I speak to Mr. Baker in room 2317, please?

Reception One moment, please. I'll put you through.
I'm sorry, there's no answer from room 2317.
Would you like to leave a message?

Guest Yes, please. My name is Henry Ford. Please tell him we are going to have a meeting tomorrow at 9 o'clock.

Reception All right, sir. I'll make sure he gets your message.
Thank you for calling.

Conversation 3 Transferring Calls within the Hotel

"Certainly, I will put you through to the restaurant."

Oliver Good afternoon, Reception, Oliver speaking.

Caller This is Julianne Moore in room 458. I'd like to reserve a table for dinner at 7 p.m. please.

Oliver Certainly, I will put you through to the restaurant.

Caller Thank you.

Oliver Please hold the line. It's ringing for you now. If your call is disconnected, please dial 27. That's the restaurant extension number.

Conversation 4 International Call

"I'd like to make an international call to Chicago."

Operator	Good morning. This is operator speaking. May I help you?
Guest	I'd like to make an international call to Chicago.
Operator	What number do you want to call?
Guest	Area code is 312 and the number is 671-954.
Operator	OK. Please hang up the phone and wait for a moment. I'll call you back as soon as your party is on the line.
Guest	Thank you.

Conversation 5 Communicating with a Caller

"I can put you through to Mr. Rogers' room."

Amy	Good evening, Sheraton Hotel, Amy speaking.
Caller	Hi, my colleague, David Rogers, is staying with you. Can you tell me which room he's staying in, please?
Amy	I'm afraid I can't give out our guests' room numbers.
Caller	well, umm, that's fine.
Amy	But I can put you through to Mr. Rogers' room. Would you like me to do that?
Caller	Yes, please.
Amy	Hold the line. I'm sorry sir. Mr. Rogers isn't in his room. Would you like to leave a message?
Caller	No, thanks. I'll try again later.

Conversation 6 Giving Information

"It is located on the 7th floor inside the fitness club."

Dylan Thank you for calling. Grand Hyatt Hotel.
How may I assist you?

Guest Hello. Do you have a swimming pool in your hotel?

Dylan Sure, we do.
It is located on the 7th floor inside the fitness club.

Guest Wonderful! How late is it open?

Dylan It is open from 8 a.m. until 10 p.m.

Guest Wow! Thank you for the information.

Dylan It's my pleasure.

Conversation 7 Dealing with Communication Problems

"I'm afraid you called the wrong hotel."

Natalia	Good morning, Raffles Hotel. What can I do for you?
Caller	May I speak to Ms. Lee in room 1611?
Natalia	Just a minute, please. I'm sorry, but Ms. Lee is not our guest at this hotel.
Caller	Oh, really? But she told me to call this hotel.
Natalia	I'm sorry, but there is no one here by that name. What number are you calling?
Caller	Isn't this Metro Hotel?
Natalia	Oh, no. This is Raffles Hotel. I'm afraid you called the wrong hotel.

Conversation 8 Explaining Services

"You can have breakfast at the restaurant in the lobby, or you can order room service."

David Good evening. May I help you?

Guest Good evening. Where can I have breakfast tomorrow?

David You can have breakfast at the restaurant in the lobby, or you can order room service.

Guest When is the restaurant open?

David The breakfast buffet is served from 6 a.m. to 11 a.m. and room service is available 24 hours.

Guest Good! thank you for your help.

David Not at all. Have a good time.

3. More Information for You

Buffet의 유래와 예절

Buffet라는 단어는 뷔페 혹은 정거장 등의 간이식당을 의미하는 단어로 발음은 미국식으로 [bəˈfeɪ] 로 읽고, 영국식 발음으로는 [ˈbʊfeɪ ; ˈbʌfeɪ] 로 발음합니다. 프랑스어로는 [byfɛ]로 발음하며 뜻은 파티 등에서 음식을 차려 놓는 식탁, 차려 놓은 음식을 의미합니다.

뷔페는 요리를 한데 모아 테이블 위에 펼쳐놓고 개인별로 원하는 음식을 가져다먹는 형태의 식사로 호텔에서는 일반적으로 breakfast buffet, brunch buffet, lunch buffet, dinner buffet 등 시간대별로 다양한 형태의 뷔페를 운영합니다.

8~10 세기경 스칸디나비아 반도의 노르만족(바이킹 Viking)들이 며칠간 배를 타고 나가 도적질을 하고 난 뒤 커다란 널빤지에 훔쳐온 각종 술과 음식을 한꺼번에 올려놓고 자축하며 먹는 식습관에서 유래하였다는 설이 전해지고 있습니다. 뷔페의 시초라 할 수 있는 스뫼르고스보르드(Smörgåsbord)는 18세기 말부터 19세기 사이에 스웨덴의 상류층에서 즐기던 요리로, 여기서 스뫼르(Smör)는 버터를 의미하여 빵에 버터를 발라 먹는다는 것을 뜻하고, 가스(gås)는 영어의 구스(goose)라는 말로 거위라는 의미하므로 가금류 구이 등의 요리가 제공된다는 것을 알 수 있습니다. 단어의 마지막에 붙은 보르드(bord)는 영어의 board로 널빤지나 식탁을 의미합니다. 스뫼르고스보르드(Smörgåsbord)를 먹는 순서는 청어요리부터 시작하여 연어, 새우 등 해산물 요리와 샐러드를 먼저 먹고 미트볼, 햄 등의 육류로 만든 요리를 먹은 뒤 치즈, 과일 등의 후식으로 마무리 합니다. 이러한 배경 때문에 아직 일본에서는 뷔페식당을 바이킹(バイキング)식당이라고 부르기도 합니다. 일각에서는 뷔페의 기원이 러시아에서 시작되었다고 주장하기도 하는데 러시아의 기후적인 특성상 겨울에 주방에서 차가운 복도를 지나 식당으로 음식을 운반하는 동안 음식이 식어버리기 때문에 아예 식당에 펼쳐 놓고 먹는 식사방법에서 시작되었다는 내용이 전해지기도 합니다.

Buffet = A buffet is a meal of cold food that is displayed on a long table at a party or public occasion. Guests usually serve themselves from the table.

최근에는 다양한 테마를 갖고 디저트 품목을 중심으로 호텔마다 뷔페 경쟁이 치열해지고 있습니다. 대표적으로 딸기를 테마로 한 딸기 뷔페가 있습니다. 봄철이 되면 서울 시내 주요 호텔들은 3만원~8만원 사이의 가격대의 딸기 뷔페를 선보이며 수많은 여성 소비자들의 여심(女心)잡기 마케팅에 앞장서고 있습니다.

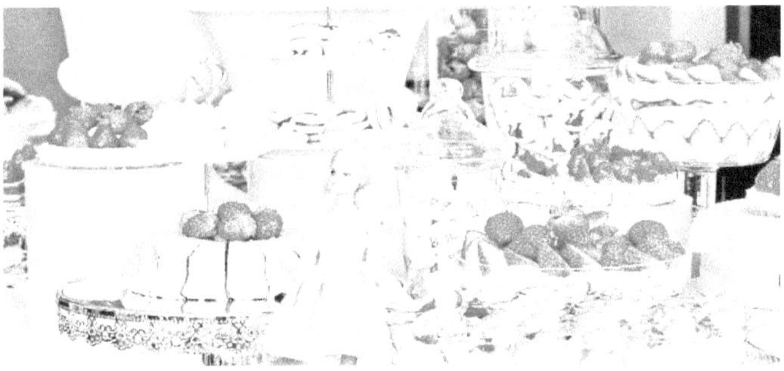

JW 메리어트 동대문 스퀘어 서울 - 살롱 드 딸기

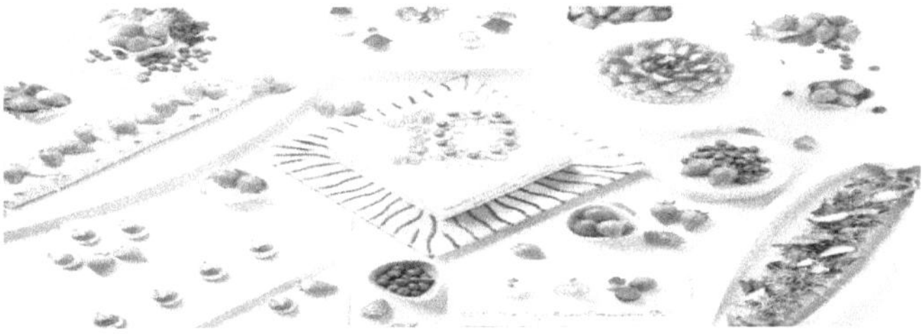

그랜드 워커힐 서울 - 베리 베리 스트로베리

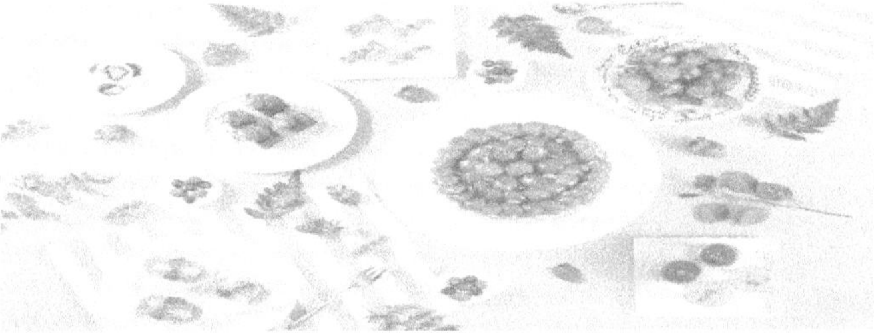

롯데호텔 서울 - 머스트 비 스트로베리

쉐라톤 서울 디큐브시티 호텔 - 올 어바웃 스트로베리

반얀트리 클럽 앤 스파 서울 - 베리 베리 베리

그랜드 인터컨티넨탈 서울 파르나스 / 인터컨티넨탈 서울 코엑스

4. DIY

Answer the following questions and do a role-play with your partner

A : This is a wake-up call for you. It's 7:30 a.m.

B :

A : Where can I get the city map?

B :

A : May I speak to Mr. Smith in room 2819?

B :

A : Would you like to leave a message?

B :

A : I'd like to reserve a table for dinner at 8 p.m. please

B :

A : I'm calling about a reservation I made last week

B :

A Story Behind the Hotel Brand

Marriott Hotels
"맥주 노점상에서 메리어트 인터내셔널이 되기까지"

윌러드 메리어트(J. Willard Marriott)는 1927년 워싱턴 D.C.에 부인 앨리스 메리어트(Alice S. Marriott)와 함께 9개의 좌석이 있는 작은 루트 비어 스탠드(음료 가판대)를 열게 됩니다. 이후 요식업으로 규모를 키워나가던 중 어느 날 지역 공항 가까운 위치에 있었던 자신의 레스토랑에서 승객들이 간단한 샌드위치와 음료를 사들고 가는 모습에서 아이디어를 얻어 이스턴 항공사에 기내식 사업을 제안하게 되고 이 기내식 서비스를 시작한 것을 계기로 호텔사업에 뛰어들면서 급성장하게 됩니다.

첫 번째 메리어트 호텔은 1957년 버지니아 주 알링턴에 오픈한 트윈 브릿지 모터 메리어트 호텔(Twin Bridge Motor Marriott Hotel)이며 이후 호텔 수를 늘려 나가며 1981년 100번째 호텔을 하와이에 오픈합니다. 메리어트 인터네셔널은 창업자 윌러드 메리어트의 이름을 딴 'JW 메리어트' 외에도 르네상스 호텔, 코트야드, 레지던스 인, 페어필드 인 앤 스위트, 스피링힐 스위트, 리츠칼튼 등과 같은 브랜드들을 포함하며 혁신과 변화를 거듭하여 미국과 전 세계 70여 국가에서 약 3400여 개의 숙박시설을 운영 중에 있습니다.

완벽주의자로 유명하였던 윌러드 메리어트는 요식사업을 하던 시절에 햄버거 패티를 몇 번 뒤집어야하는지 매뉴얼화시킬 정도로 서비스 표준화를 중시하였습니다. 호텔 사업이 본격화되면서 그는 호텔 내의 작은 부분까지도 모두 매뉴얼을 만들어 직원들을 철저하게 교육시켰으며 '직원이 가장 중요한 자산'이라는 신념을 지켜내며 철저한 서비스의 체계화와 표준화를 확립합니다. 1972년 CEO로 취임한 이래 39년간 같은 자리를 지켜온 그의 아들 빌 메리어트 주니어 역시 아버지로부터 경영철학을 물려받아 '경영자가 직원을 잘 챙기면 직원은 고객에게 최선을 다하게 되며 결국 고객은 다시 우리 호텔을 찾게 된다.'는 신조를 갖고 호텔 업계의 제왕이 되었습니다. 빌 메리어트 주니어는 직원 및 고객과 직접 소통하기 위하여 75세 때 블로그를 만들어 운영하기도 하고 해마다 국내외의 호텔 체인을 직접 돌아다니는 열정적인 CEO로서 메리어트의 또 다른 역사 일부를 장식하며 2011년 퇴임하였습니다.

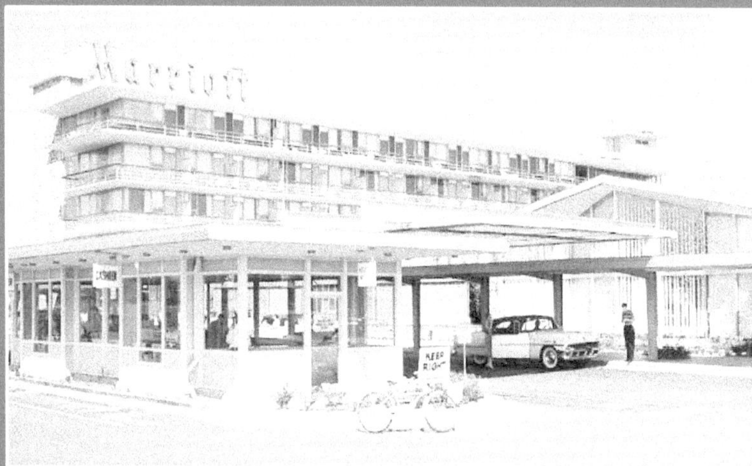

[Twin Bridge Motor Marriott Hotel]

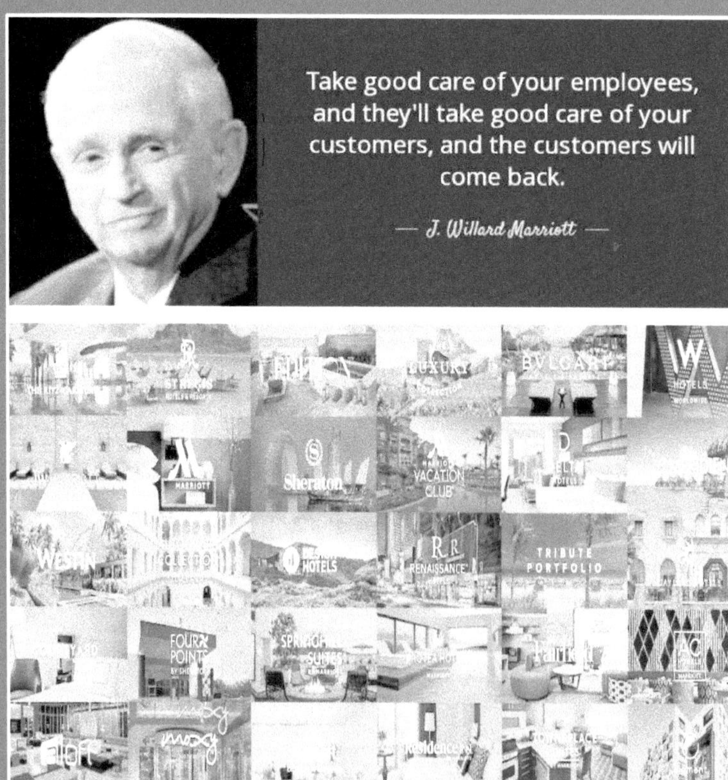

[Marriott International]

Unit
6

Food and Beverage Service

We will learn
- how to welcome diners
- how to take orders
- how to handle payment

Hotel English

1. What They Do

호텔 식음료 서비스(Food and Beverage Service)는 고객에게 음식과 음료를 제공하기 위하여 접대시설을 갖추고 이윤추구를 목적으로 인적 · 물적 서비스를 제공하는 것을 의미합니다. 호텔 식음료 서비스는 유형의 식음료 상품과 무형의 인적 서비스 그리고 기타 여러 가지 요소들이 결합된 형태이며, 식음료부서의 업무 흐름도는 다음과 같습니다.

메뉴 기획 → 메뉴 레시피 작성 → 식자재 주문 → 식자재 발주 → 식자재 입고 및 저장 → 식자재의 주방 반출 → 상품 생산 → 상품 판매 → 고객 피드백 → 메뉴 기획

식음료 주문받는 요령

- 고객 착석 후 환영인사와 함께 시계방향으로 1인 1매 메뉴판 제공
- 메뉴는 고객의 우측에서 전달하고 주문 받을 때는 고객의 좌측에 위치
- 주문기록은 주문서에 통일된 약자로 정확히 기재하며 주문내용 재확인
- 주문받을 시 양발을 모으고 양팔은 겨드랑이에 자연스럽게 붙이며 허리를 약 15도 숙이고 고객의 얼굴을 주시하면서 공손한 태도 유지
- 주문받는 순서는 시계방향으로 여자, 남자, hostess, host 순으로 받음
- 조리시간이 오래 소요되는 요리에 대해서는 주문 받을 시 반드시 별도 안내
- 음식과 어울리는 주류나 음료를 추천
- 요리는 고객의 오른쪽에서 제공하고 왼쪽에서 정리

2. Conversations

Conversation 1 Escorting Diners

"There's a vegetarian menu on the back of the menu."

Restaurant	Good evening, sir. Welcome to the restaurant. May I take your coats?
Guest	Yes, please. Thank you.
Restaurant	Do you have a reservation?
Guest	Yes, I do. I reserved a table for two under my name, Ted Collins.
Restaurant	All right, sir. Would you like to sit by the window?
Guest	No, I want a table in a quiet corner. I'm having an important business meeting.
Restaurant	Very well, sir. Would you come this way, sir?
Guest	Thank you.
Restaurant	How do you like this table?
Guest	Great. I'll take a seat here. And can I have a vegetarian menu? I'm a vegan.
Restaurant	There's a vegetarian menu on the back of the menu. 'Tofu Salad' is a recommended vegetarian menu. It consists of greens and tofu with oriental dressing. You can change the dressing when you order.
Guest	It sounds so nice.
Restaurant	Please let me know when you're ready to order.

Conversation 2 Welcoming Guests

"Would you like an aperitif before you order?"

Restaurant	Good evening sir, madam. How are you this evening?
Guest 1	I'm good. Thank you.
Restaurant	Would you like an aperitif before you order?
Guest 1	Yes, please.
Guest 2	I'm going to have some wine first.
Restaurant	Here's the wine list. There are many different kinds of wines and on the last page you'll see the full wine list.
Guest 2	That's wonderful. Thank you.
Restaurant	I will come back to take your order in a few minutes.
	(Few moments later)
Guest 1	Excuse me, I think we are ready to order now.
Restaurant	Ok, what can I get you, sir?
Guest 1	I'd like the sirloin steak with mashed potatoes, please.
Restaurant	Sure. How would you like your steak?
Guest 1	Medium rare, please.
Restaurant	And what are you going to have, madam?
Guest 2	I'll have roasted rack of lamb with mustard sauce, please.
Restaurant	Excellent choices. I'll be back with your dishes. Thank you.

Conversation 3 Taking Drinks Orders

"What would you like to drink?"

Bar Good evening, sir. What would you like to drink?

Guest I'll have a martini.

Bar Would you like that straight up or on the rocks?

Guest 1 Make it a shot of whisky on the rocks, please.

Bar What brand whisky would you like?

Guest 1 The best you have.

Bar What can I get you, ma'am?

Guest 2 I'd like a beer, please.

Bar Would you like draught or bottled beer?

Guest 2 I'd like to try a local bottled beer.
What would you recommend?

Bar Well, the Castello and Antoniano are the most popular one.

Guest 2 Then I will have an Antoniano, please.

Bar There you are. Is there anything else you need?

Guest 1 Can I have some nuts and corn chips?

Bar No problem. I will be right back with them.

Conversation 4 Taking Orders at the Bar

"What can I get you today?"

Bar Good afternoon, sir. How are you?

Guest Fine, thanks.

Bar What can I get you today?

Guest Two gin and tonics, please.

Bar Ok, would you like a slice of lemon?

Guest Yes, please.

Bar Here you are. Would you like to pay them now or shall I start a tab for you?

Guest I think we'll start a tab.
We might have another drink later on.

Bar Of course. Could you give me your room number, please?

Guest I'm in 514.

Bar Could you sign here, please?

Guest Sure, thank you.

Conversation 5 Taking Breakfast Orders

"We are offering an American Breakfast buffet."

Restaurant	Good morning. Can I have your room number, please?
Guest	Good morning. I'm in room 703.
Restaurant	Thank you. We are offering an American Breakfast buffet. Feel free to help yourselves. Can I bring you some tea or coffee?
Guest	Coffee for me and tea for her, please.
Restaurant	Here you are. Here's your coffee and tea. Would you like anything from the menu?
Guest	I'd like to order some eggs.
Restaurant	How would you like your eggs?
Guest	Sunny-side up, please.
Restaurant	Here you are. Is there anything else I can get you?
Guest	No, thanks.
Restaurant	Enjoy your breakfast.

Conversation 6 Asking about Food and Dessert

"What would you like to have for dessert?"

Restaurant Good afternoon, sir. Can I take your order now?

Guest Would you give me a glass of beer while I'm deciding?

Restaurant Sure, sir.

(returning with a glass of beer a little later)

Restaurant Have you decided what to order?

Guest Yes. I'd like some beef curry and rice.

Restaurant All right. We serve a small salad with the beef curry. What kind of dressing would you like to have?

Guest French dressing, please.

(after finishing meal)

Restaurant Excuse me, may I clear away your plates?

Guest Yes. We're finished.

Restaurant How did you like your meal?

Guest It was very delicious.

Restaurant I'm glad you liked the food. What would you like to have for dessert?

Guest I will have a slice of cheese cake and a cappuccino, please.

Restaurant Certainly. Let me serve your dessert right away.

Conversation 7 Handling Payment

"How will you be paying?"

Guest Can I have the check, please? I'd like to pay my bill now.

Restaurant Just a moment, please. Here is your check.

Guest Is the service charge included?

Restaurant Yes. A 10% service charge is included in the bill. How will you be paying?

Guest I am going to charge it to my room.

Restaurant All right, ma'am. Please sign here and write your room number here.

Guest Sure. Here it is.

Restaurant Thank you very much. It was my pleasure to serve you today.

3. More Tips For You

Types of Breakfast Egg

Ⓐ sunny-side up

Ⓑ over easy egg

Ⓒ over hard egg

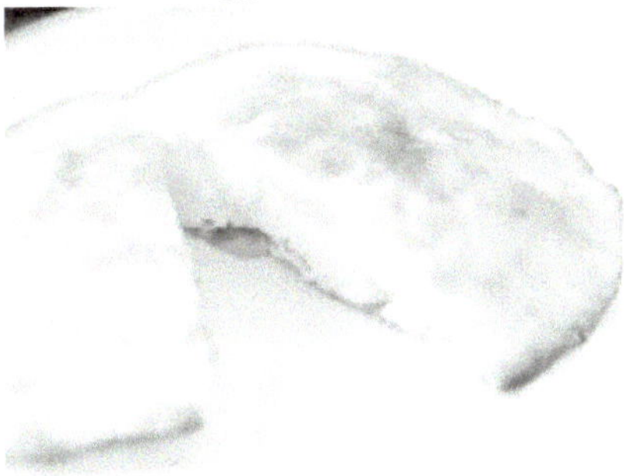

Ⓓ scrambled egg

Ⓔ omelette

Ⓕ poached egg

Degrees of Steak Doneness

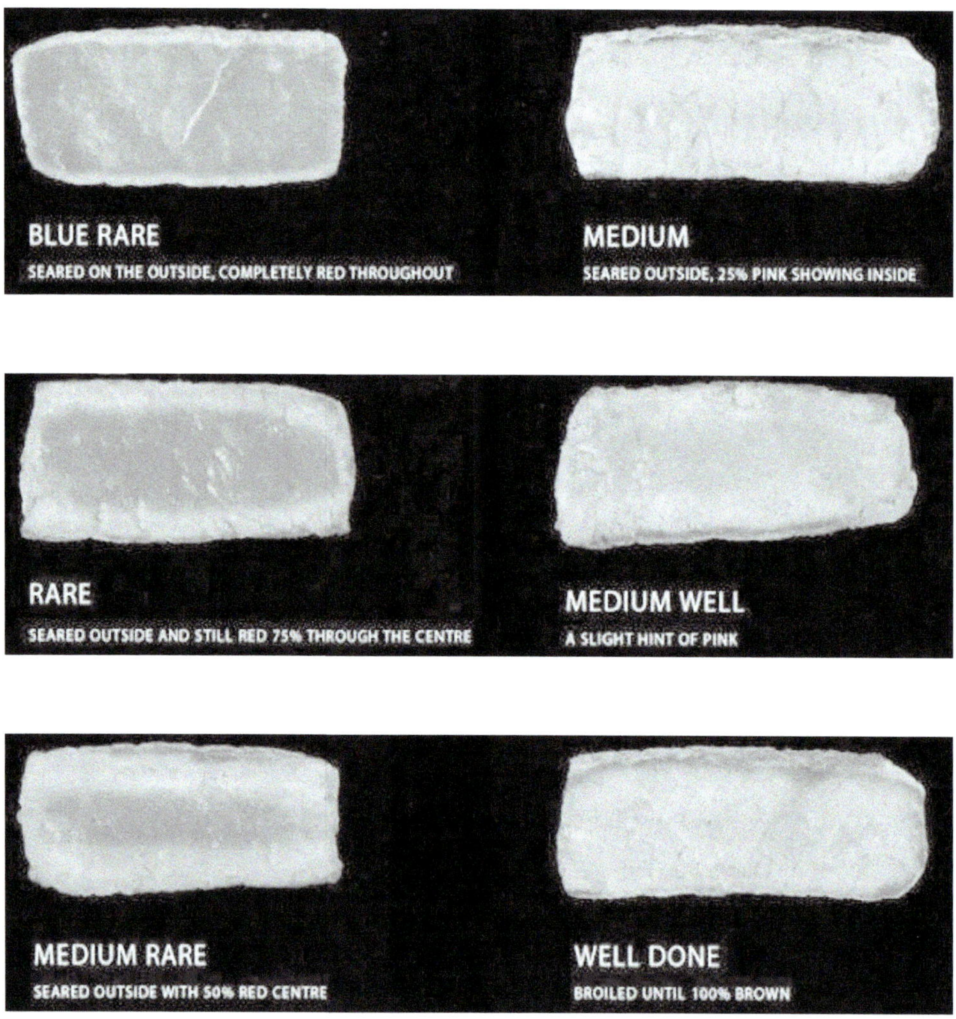

4. DIY

Put the words in the sentences into the correct order

(1) take coats your I may

→

(2) you can aperitif bring I an

→

(3) menus give me let some you

→

(4) order me to know are you when let ready

→

(5) the list wine would see like to you

→

(6) a moments come few in your back I'll order take to

→

A Story Behind the Hotel Brand

Waldorf Astoria Hotels and Resorts
"뉴욕의 왕궁 월도프 아스토리아"

월도프 아스토리아 호텔은 윌리엄 월도프 아스토가 1893년 세운 월도프 호텔과 1892년에 세운 아스토리아 호텔을 합쳐 1931년 10월 문을 연 당시 세계 최고의 호텔이었습니다. 1949년 콘래드 힐튼 창업주가 이 호텔을 인수하게 되고 2014년 10월 중국 안방보험그룹(安邦保險)에 매각되었으나 향후 100년 동안 힐튼월드와 이드가 호텔 운영을 지속하기로 하였습니다.
월도프 아스토리아 호텔 탄생 배경에 얽힌 유명한 일화가 오늘날까지 회자되고 있는데 그 내용은 다음과 같습니다.
폭우가 내리던 어느 밤, 노부부는 하룻밤 머무를 만한 숙소를 찾아 헤매던 중 필라델피아의 허름하고 작은 호텔에 들어가게 됩니다. 그러나 당시 도시 내에 큰 행사가 열리던 기간이라 빈방이 없었고 이 노부부를 맞이한 호텔 직원은 인근 호텔들까지 알아봤으나 빈 객실을 찾지 못했습니다. 이 호텔 직원은 자신의 방을 내주며 하룻밤 머무를 수 있도록 친절을 베풀었고 노부부는 감사한 마음에 다음 날 아침 호텔을 떠나며 객실료의 3배를 건넸으나 그는 객실이 아닌 직원방을 잠깐 내어준 것이므로 돈을 받을 수 없다며 극구 사양했습니다. 2년이 지난 뒤 어느 날 노부부는 이 호텔 직원에게 뉴욕행 항공권과 초대장을 보냈고 호텔 직원은 휴가를 내어 초대받은 호텔로 향했습니다. 이제 막 오픈한 화려한 호텔에서 그를 맞이한 노부부는 당신을 위해 이 호텔을 지었다며 호텔 경영을 제안합니다. 이 호텔 직원이 바로 월도프 아스토리아 호텔의 초대 경영자이자 세계 굴지의 호텔 체인을 이룩한 조지 볼트(George Bolt)이며, 이 일화는 진정한 환대정신이란 무엇인가에 대한 답을 제시해주고 있습니다.

[Waldorf Astoria Hotel]

[George Bolt]

Unit 7

Room Service

We will learn
- how to take room service orders
- how to explain room service menus
- how to deliver room service

Hotel English

1. What They Do

룸서비스는 고객이 객실에서 메뉴를 주문한 뒤 주문한 식사를 객실에서 할 수 있도록 해주는 서비스입니다. 룸서비스는 투숙객을 대상으로 제공되는 서비스이기 때문에 24시간 주문 대기를 해야 하며, 최근에는 In Room Dining 으로 불리기도 합니다. 사적인 영역을 중시하는 문화가 확산됨에 따라 룸서비스는 호텔 제공 서비스 중 중요한 일부가 되어가고 있습니다. 오더테이커(order taker)가 객실 고객으로부터 전화나 door knob으로 메뉴를 주문받아 객실까지 식음료를 제공하기도 하고 객실 이외의 호텔 내 시설에서 고객의 주문이 있으면 이 역시 룸서비스 부서에서 전담하여 고객에서 서비스를 제공합니다.

룸서비스는 레스토랑 서비스보다 더 많은 노동력과 전문성이 요구되므로 가격이 더 비싸다는 특성이 있지만 고객의 입장에서는 24시간 언제든지 원하는 시간에 맞춰 원하는 메뉴를 제공받을 수 있다는 편리성 때문에 룸서비스를 많이 이용하고 있습니다.

룸서비스의 특성

- 중식, 양식, 일식, 한식, 기타 스낵 종류까지 다양한 메뉴 주문이 가능
- 호텔 투숙객이나 기타 시설 이용객을 대상으로 연중 24시간 운영
- 전화를 이용한 주문이 대부분이므로 정확한 커뮤니케이션이 중요
- 특히 전화를 통한 주문의 경우, 주문을 받은 후 주문내용을 반복해서 철저히 확인
- 음식이 준비되면 트롤리를 이용하여 전용 엘리베이터를 타고 객실까지 서빙

2. Conversations

Conversation 1 Taking Room Service Orders

"Room Service, How may I help you?"

Room Service	Room Service, How may I help you?
Guest	Can I order some room service?
Room Service	Of course, sir. Could I have your room number, please?
Guest	It's 912. Mr. Smith.
Room Service	What would like, Mr. Smith?
Guest	I'd like an American Breakfast.
Room Service	Ok, would you like tea or coffee?
Guest	Coffee, please. Could I have an espresso?
Room Service	Certainly, sir.
Guest	How long will that be? I'm in a hurry this morning.
Room Service	It will be with you in 15 minutes.
Guest	Sounds perfect.

Conversation 2 Solving Problems

"You can find a menu in the drawer of your side table."

Room Service	May I help you?
Guest	I'd like to order breakfast in my room. I need to see the menu, first. Would you please send the menu to my room?
Room Service	You can find a menu in the drawer of your side table.
Guest	Oh, really? Yes, I've found it. Let me see. I need some time to decide. Can I call you back to order in 10 minutes?
Room Service	Sure, take your time and let us know when you're ready.

Conversation 3 Breakfast Orders

"I'd like to have a continental breakfast for two."

Room Service	Good morning, Room Service. How can I help you?
Guest	This is room 1509. I'd like to have a continental breakfast for two.
Room Service	Continental for two. What kind of juice do you want?
Guest	One orange juice and one tomato juice.
Room Service	All right, ma'am.
Guest	How long will it be?
Room Service	It will take 10 to 15 minutes.
Guest	Great. Thank you very much.

Conversation 4 Explaining Menus

"How would you like your burger cooked?"

Room Service: Good afternoon. Room Service.
How can I help you?

Guest: I'd like to order some room service.
What is today's soup?

Room Service: It's a potato-based Boston clam chowder, sir.

Guest: Then we'll have two bowls of today's soup, a cheeseburger and a BLT sandwich, please.

Room Service: How would you like your burger cooked?

Guest: Medium well done, please. Does it come with French fries?

Room Service: Of course, yes. Anything to drink?

Guest: One coke and one sprite, please.

Room Service: I see. Your order will be up within 20 minutes. Thank you.

Conversation 5 Agreeing Delivery Times

"What time do you want it served?"

Guest	This is Mrs. Baker calling from 1108. May I have dinner delivered to my room?
Room Service	Okay. What would you like, ma'am?
Guest	Two T-bone steaks, and two glasses of red wine, please.
Room Service	How would you like your steak?
Guest	Medium rare, please.
Room Service	Would you like some soup or salad?
Guest	One chicken salad with Italian dressing.
Room Service	What would you like for dessert?
Guest	Apple pudding and peppermint tea, please.
Room Service	Is there anything else?
Guest	No, that's it.
Room Service	What time do you want it served?
Guest	At 6:30, please.
Room Service	Thank you. The server will be up at that time.

Conversation 6 Delivering Room Service

"I've brought the dinner you ordered."

(ringing the door bell)

Room Service	Room Service.
Guest	Please come in.
Room Service	Good evening, sir. I've brought the dinner you ordered. Where would you like to eat?
Guest	Could you put it on the table by the window?
Room Service	Yes, sir. Here you are.
Guest	That looks delicious. Thank you very much.
Room Service	You're welcome. Enjoy your meal.

Conversation 7 Apologizing for Mistakes

"I'm afraid there must have been a mistake."

Room Service Room Service. May I come in?

Guest Please come on in.

Room Service I brought the lunch you ordered.

Guest Could you set up a table over there, please?

Room Service Certainly. Here you are. Is there anything else you need, ma'am?

Guest Well, I don't see my drinks. I ordered two sodas.

Room Service Oh, let me check your order slip. I'm really sorry, ma'am.
I'm afraid there must have been a mistake.
I'll be right back with your drinks.

Guest Okay, thanks.

3. More Tips For You

American Breakfast vs. Continental Breakfast

American Breakfast

미국식 조식은 일반적으로 계절과일(Season Fruit), 주스류(Juice), 시리얼(Cereal), 계란요리(Eggs), 음료(Beverage), 케이크류(Cake), 빵종류(Bread & Rolls), 햄 베이컨 혹은 소시지 등이 곁들여 제공됩니다.

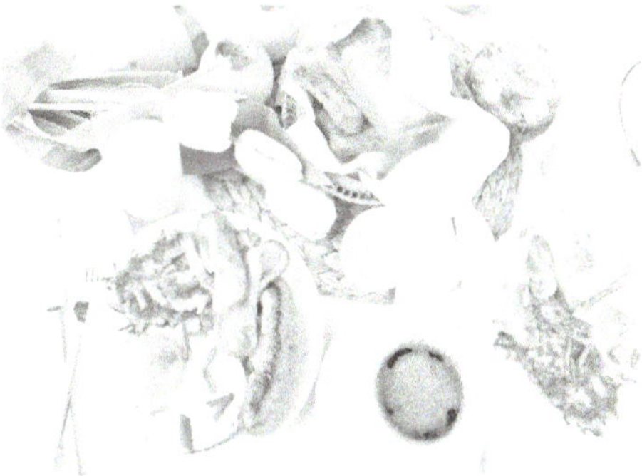

Continental Breakfast

유럽식 조식은 간단하게 빵, 버터와 잼, 주스, 커피 또는 차 등으로 구성되며 미국식 조식과 달리 계란, 햄, 베이컨, 소시지 등이 제공되지 않습니다.

4. DIY

You have to take room service orders. Please complete the following conversation.

You : (Answer phone by saying department and your name)

Guest : Good morning. Is it too early to order some room service?

You : (Tell guest it is not too early and ask what the caller wants)

Guest : Could I have a sandwich with fresh fruit juice?

You : (Reply polite and ask guest what kind of juice)

Guest : I'll have a grapefruit juice, please

You : (Ask guest if the guest need anything else)

Guest : That's it. How long will that be?

You : (Tell guest about 15 minutes and end call politely)

A Story Behind the Hotel Brand

Raffles Hotel
"See You at Raffles"

아르메니아 사람인 사르키에스 4형제는 페르시아에서 싱가포르로 이주했습니다. 당시 수에즈 운하 개통으로 영국과 싱가포르를 이어주는 항로가 급증했기 때문에 숙박시설의 수요가 늘어날 것이라고 예상한 형제는 1884년 말레이시아 페낭에 이스턴 호텔(Eastern Hotel)을 세우고, 이어서 오리엔탈 호텔(Oriental Hotel)도 개관합니다. 이를 토대로 오래된 방갈로를 인수하여 1887년 12월 객실 수가 10개인 래플스호텔(Raffles Hotel)을 탄생시킵니다. 이는 싱가포르에서 가장 오래된 호텔이며, 동양에 몇 남지 않은 19세기 호텔 중 하나이기도 합니다. 래플스호텔은 스탬퍼드 래플스(Stamford Raffles)라는 영국의 식민지 담당 정치가이자 싱가포르 건설자인 그의 이름을 따서 지어진 이름입니다.

화려한 네오르네상스 장식, 프론트에 최초로 설치한 전기 조명, 첫 프랑스인 셰프 등 래플스 호텔은 최고급 호텔로 승승장구하며 유럽 상류층으로부터 '동양의 진주', '수에즈 운하 동쪽에서 가장 영향력 있는 장소' 등의 수식어를 얻게 됩니다. 1920년대에는 "see you at Raffles!"라는 말이 유행처럼 번질 정도로 상류층 사이에서 최고의 사교 문화 공간이 됩니다.

그러나 1920년대 대공황과 1933년 막내 아르사이크가 사망하는 등 사르키에스 형제는 전설 속에서 사라지게 됩니다. 수많은 변화를 거쳐 1987년 싱가포르 국립 기념물로 지정된 후, 1991년 9월 16일 최초의 래플스를 닮은 모습으로 다시 오픈하게 됩니다. 예전의 래플스를 그리워하는 오래된 단골 고객들은 새로워진 래플스를 반기지 않았고 단골 고객들만의 사적인 분위기도 사라지게 되었지만 그럼에도 불구하고 지금까지도 래플스만의 전통과 명성을 유지하고 있습니다. 래플스호텔에서는 고객을 게스트가 아닌 레지던트라고 부르는데 그만큼 고객들이 내 집 같은 편안함을 느낄 수 있도록 세심한 부분까지 신경을 쓰는 것으로 유명합니다.

[Raffles Hotel]

[Raffles Hotel Room]

Unit 8

Concierge

We will learn
- how to check information for guests
- how to make recommendations
- how to find solutions to problems

Hotel English

1. What They Do

컨시어지는 고객이 머무는 동안 불편함을 느끼지 못하도록 고객이 원하는 모든 업무를 수행해주는 역할을 하는 부서입니다. 호텔 내 각 시설의 영업시간, 이용 가능한 시설, 행사 등 호텔과 관련된 정보뿐 아니라 고객이 필요로 하는 개인적인 요구사항까지 해결해줄 수 있어야 하기 때문에 항상 새로운 지식을 습득하고 외국어소통능력도 뛰어나야 합니다.

컨시어지의 업무는 매우 광범위하고 다양한데 예를 들면 항공편 예약, 호텔 근처 유명 레스토랑 추천 및 예약, 공연 예약, 전시회 안내, 관광지 안내, 우편물 접수 및 발송 등이 있습니다. 컨시어지 업무는 일부 호텔에서는 VIP고객 서비스를 전담하는 GRO(Guest Relationship Office)팀에서 대신 수행하기도 합니다.

컨시어지와 GRO의 차이점은?

GRO(Guest Relationship Officer)는 컨시어지와 비슷한 역할이지만 서비스를 제공하는 대상이 다릅니다. 컨시어지가 일반 고객을 대상으로 비서업무를 수행한다면 GRO는 VIP고객을 대상으로 호텔 내외부 안내, 체크인, 객실 안내, 상담, 영접, 영송 등의 업무를 수행합니다.

2. Conversations

Conversation 1 What to Eat

"Can you recommend a good Korean restaurant?"

Guest: I'd like to have some Korean food.
Can you recommend a good Korean restaurant?

Concierge: Well, the most famous one in this city is the Han Kook Jib but it gets very busy. On Friday nights you usually have to make reservations.
It has some good real Korean food.

Guest: I've already been there before. This time I'd like to go to another place outside the hotel.

Concierge: If you want to try another place, there is a Korean restaurant called Gaya within a 10-minute walk.

Guest: How is the food there?

Concierge: They are very proud of their Korean meat dishes such as Bulgogi and Galbi. I'm sure you'll love it.

Guest: Oh, that's nice. I love meat dish so much.
Could you make reservations for us?

Concierge: You don't usually need reservations.

Guest: Ok, can you show us where it is on a map?

Concierge: Of course. I'll explain the location with the map

Conversation 2 How to Go

"Would you suggest some places to buy Korean traditional things?"

Concierge Good morning, ma'am. How may I help you?

Guest I want to buy some gifts for my family. Would you suggest some places to buy Korean traditional things?

Concierge Of course, ma'am. You should go to Namdaemoon Market or Insadong area. There are lots of shops where they are selling a variety of Korean traditional souvenirs.

Guest Can I visit them by subway?

Concierge Certainly. Here is a map of Seoul and a map of subway is on the back. You'll see the subway station right in front of the hotel.

Guest Thanks a lot.

Concierge My pleasure.

Conversation 3 Lost and Found

"Let me check the list of lost items."

Guest I lost my wallet somewhere in the lobby.
Could it be in your Lost and Found?

Concierge I'm sorry to hear that, sir.
Could you describe your wallet for me?

Guest It is a black leather one. It has a big letter Y on the front.

Concierge Hold on a second. Let me check the list of lost items.
Oh, here it is. Is this yours?

Guest Oh, there it is. Oh, my god, you are a lifesaver.
The wallet is very meaningful to me.
I really appreciate it.

Concierge You're welcome. I'm so glad you got your wallet back.

Conversation 4 Where to Visit

"What kind of place would you like to visit?"

Concierge How can I help you?

Guest Yes, let me ask you something.

Concierge Sure. Go ahead.

Guest I'd like to do some sightseeing in Seoul. Would you recommend some famous places to visit?

Concierge What kind of place would you like to experience?

Guest Well, I'm interested in Korean history and culture.

Concierge Then you had better visit Gyeongbokgung, the main royal palace of Chosun Dynasty. If you go there, you can also visit the Korean traditional museum.

Guest Great! Where is it located?

Concierge It is very near from the hotel, so you can walk there. If you want more detailed information, you can get a leaflet in front of the information desk.

Guest I see. Thank you very much.

Conversation 5 What to See

"Would you recommend some good concerts or shows?"

Concierge	Good morning, sir. How may I help you?
Guest	I'd like to go to one of the Korean famous theatres. Would you recommend some good concerts or shows?
Concierge	Oh, you can go to the Korean classical music concert at Seoul Art Hall next to our hotel this evening.
Guest	That sounds good. Could you get us the tickets?
Concierge	Sure. How many tickets do you want, sir?
Guest	Four, please. How much is the ticket?
Concierge	It is fifteen thousand won.

Conversation 6 Rent a Car

"Let me check with a rent-a-car service."

Guest	Will you do me a favor?
Concierge	Yes, sir. How can I help you?
Guest	My friends are coming from Canada and we need a car and a driver to take us to some places.
Concierge	When do you need them, sir?
Guest	This coming weekend.
Concierge	Let me check with a rent-a-car service. What type of vehicle do you want?
Guest	We are all five, so I'd like a van and an English speaking driver.
Concierge	All right, sir. I'll try my best.

3. More Tips For You

오늘날 외국인 관광객들이 많이 찾는 대부분의 식당에서는 영어메뉴판을 구비해 놓고 있으며 내국인을 대상으로 하는 일반 식당에서도 영문 음식명을 동시에 표기하고 있습니다. 그러나 표준화되지 않아서 식당마다 다른 영문 음식명을 사용한다거나 잘못된 영어표현을 사용함에 따라 관광객들에게 많은 혼란을 주기도 합니다.

음식에 대한 이해도를 높이고 영문 음식명 표준화를 위하여 문화체육관광부와 농림수산식품부, 전문가들의 의견을 모아 대표적인 한식 200가지에 대한 영어, 일어, 중국어 표준안을 발표하였습니다.

번호	음식명	로마자 표기	영어 번역
1	한정식	Han-jeongsik	Korean Table d'hote
2	곤드레나물밥	Gondeure-namul-bap	Seasoned Thistle with Rice
3	김밥	Gimbap	Gimbap
4	김치볶음밥	Kimchi-bokkeum-bap	Kimchi Fried Rice
5	낙지덮밥	Nakji-deopbap	Spicy Stir-fied Octopus with rice
6	누룽지	Nurungji	Scorched Rice
7	돌솥비빔밥	Dolsot-bibimbap	Hot Stone Pot Bibimbap
8	돼지국밥	Dwaji-gukbap	Pork and Rice soup
9	밥	Bap	Rice
10	보리밥	Bori-bap	Barley Rice
11	불고기덮밥	Bulgogi-deopbap	Bulgogi with Rice
12	비빔밥	Bibimbap	Bibimbap
13	산채비빔밥	Sanchae-bibimbap	Wild Vegetable Bibimbap
14	새싹비빔밥	Saessak-bibimbap	Sprout Bibimbap
15	소고기국밥	So-gogi-gukbap	Beef and Rice Soup
16	순댓국밥	Sundae-gukbap	Korean Sausage and Rice soup
17	너비아니	Neobiani	Marinated Grilled Beef Slices
18	닭갈비	Dak-galbi	Spice Stir-fried chicken
19	불고기	Bulggogi	Bulgogi
20	삼겹살	Samgyeop-sal	Grilled Pork Belly

4. DIY

Complete these sentences with words from the box

of for out up in on per at

① Take the elevator _____ to the second floor

② I need to print something _____

③ I will take care _____ that for you

④ The fitness center opens _____ May

⑤ I will check the flight schedule _____ the Internet

⑥ What can I do _____ you?

⑦ The plug on my lead doesn't fit _____ this socket

⑧ French restaurant is _____ the third floor

⑨ You can use the facilities free _____ charge

⑩ Would you look something _____ for me?

A Story Behind the Hotel Brand

호텔과 패션의 상관관계
"호텔을 통한 패션브랜드의 아이덴티티 표현"

브랜드 인지도를 탄탄히 다져온 패션 브랜드들이 호텔 사업으로 그 영역을 확장하고 있습니다. 위험성이 따르기도 하지만 기존 호텔 브랜드보다 인지도 높은 패션 브랜드가 기획한 호텔은 참신하고 큰 화제를 몰고 등장하기 때문에 앞으로도 패션 브랜드들의 호텔 진출은 계속 이어질 전망입니다. 기존에 패션 안에서만 브랜드 아이덴티티를 표현해야했다면 호텔을 통하여 브랜드의 또 다른 가치를 표현해볼 수도 있고 만약 호텔이용을 계기로 그 브랜드에 호감을 갖게 되었다면 향후 해당 브랜드 구매까지 이어질 수 있는 효과도 있습니다. 호텔운영에 필요한 하드웨어와 소프트웨어만 탄탄히 갖춰진다면 앞으로 패션 브랜드와 호텔 산업과는 더욱 밀접한 관계에 놓일 것으로 보입니다.

대표적인 명품 브랜드 루이비통의 정식 명칭인 루이비통 모에 헤네시(Louis Vuitton Moet Hennessy, LVMH)가 2012년프랑스의 쿠르슈벨에 하이엔드급 리조트 호텔인 르슈발 블랑(Le Cheval Blanc)을 오픈하여 운영 중이며, 페라가모는 1995년 이탈리아 피렌체에 룬가르노 호텔(Lungarno hotel)을 오픈하여 현재 피렌체를 중심으로 호텔 7개와 아파트먼트, 빌라 등을 운영 중입니다. 아르마니 역시 2010년에 세계에서 가장 높은 건물로 알려진 두바이의 부르즈 할리파(Burj Khalifa)에 아르마니 호텔 1호점을 개관한 이후 2011년에는 이탈리아의 밀라노에 아르마니 호텔 밀라노(Armani Hotel Milano)를 오픈하였습니다. 이탈리아의 대표적인 보석 브랜드 불가리가 2001년 매리어트 인터네셔널과 손을 잡고 불가리 호텔 앤 리조트(Bulgari Hotels & Resorts)를 탄생시켰고 이어서 2007년에는 발리의 울루와뚜에 고급 리조트 형태의 불가리 호텔 앤 리조트 발리(Bulgari Hotels & Resorts Bali)를 성공시키며 불가리의 스타일로 재해석한 호텔 라이프 문화를 만들어 가고 있습니다. 이 외에도 모스키노, 미쏘니, 디젤, 베르사체 등이 저마다의 개성과 정체성을 담아 다양한 형태의 호텔을 운영 중이며 당분간 패션 브랜드들의 호텔업 진출은 지속될 것으로 예상됩니다.

[ARMANI Hotel Dubai]

[BVLGARI Hotel London]

[Hotel MISSONI Edinburg]

Unit 9

Housekeeping

We will learn
- how to deal with requests
- how to solve housekeeping problems
- how to handle guests' complaints

Hotel English

1. What They Do

하우스키핑은 호텔 객실의 청소와 객실 시설관리 뿐 아니라 연회장, 식음료업장, 회의실, 복도, 현관, 화장실, 주방, 정원 등과 같은 공공시설의 정비와 린넨 관리·수선 그리고 고객의 세탁물 서비스까지 담당하고 있는 부서입니다.
호텔의 객실 상품은 하우스키핑 부서를 거쳐 새로운 상품으로 재탄생되므로 하우스키핑 부서는 각종 업무를 신속하고 기능적으로 관리하여 객실을 항상 청결하고 정돈된 상태로 유지해야 합니다.
하우스키핑 부서의 주요 업무는 다음과 같습니다.

- 고객이 청결하고 편안하게 체류할 수 있는 객실 환경 조성
- 객실을 포함한 호텔 내·외부 시설의 청결 유지와 관리
- 객실의 설비, 가구, 비품류의 정비
- 객실용 린넨과 소모품 관리
- 객실 내 미니바 제공 및 서비스
- 객실 내 습득물 관리 서비스
- 식음료 업장 린넨과 유니폼 관리 업무
- 타부서와의 협조를 통한 호텔 공공부문의 재산관리 및 정비

일반적으로 객실은 다음과 같은 순위에 의해서 정비됩니다.

① 고객이 청소를 요구할 때
② VIP룸은 가능한 오전 중에 마무리
③ 체크아웃 완료된 객실
④ 고객이 투숙 중인 객실
⑤ 체크아웃 예정인 객실
⑥ 당일 예약하여 체크인하는 VIP룸

2. Conversations

Conversation 1 Solving Housekeeping Problems

"I'll send a maid up as soon as I can, madam."

Housekeeping	Good morning, Housekeeping. Maria Speaking.
Guest	Is that Housekeeping?
Housekeeping	Yes, it is. How can I help you?
Guest	I've just come back to room 249 and my room hasn't been cleaned. The breakfast dishes haven't been taken away and the bed hasn't been made. What a letdown!
Housekeeping	Oh, I'm very sorry, madam.
Guest	And I need some extra pillows.
Housekeeping	How many pillows do you need, ma'am?
Guest	Can I have four extra ones, please?
Housekeeping	Certainly, madam. I'll send a maid up as soon as I can.

Conversation 2 Laundry Service

"I have some laundry."

Housekeeping	Good afternoon! How may I help you?
Guest	My room is 1225. I have some laundry. Can you send someone to pick them up?
Housekeeping	All right, sir. I'll have somebody come up to your room now.
Guest	Thank you.
	(a few minutes later)
	(knocking on the door)
Housekeeping	Hello, laundry service.
Guest	Yes, come in, please. These shirts and pants need washing and ironing. And I want this suit dry-cleaned.
Housekeeping	Yes, sir. When do you want to get them back?
Guest	Can you deliver it by noon tomorrow?
Housekeeping	Certainly, sir. Did you fill out the laundry slip?
Guest	Yes, I did. And charge it to my room, please.
Housekeeping	Yes, sir. No problem.

Conversation 3 Dealing with Requests

"I need a towel and a few more hangers."

Housekeeping	This is housekeeping. May I help you?
Guest	This is room 1327. I need a towel and a few more hangers.
Housekeeping	Absolutely, ma'am. What kind of towel do you need?
Guest	A body towel, please.
Housekeeping	I'll send someone up there with a towel and four hangers right away.
Guest	Thank you.

Conversation 4 Make Up Room

"Can you make up my room?"

Housekeeping	Good morning, sir. May I help you?
Guest	Yes, I need my room cleaned up. I'm going out now. Can you make up my room?
Housekeeping	What's your room number, sir?
Guest	My room number is 807.
Housekeeping	Yes, sir. A room maid will be there in 10 minutes.
Guest	By the way, I have left many papers on the desk. Please tell her not to move them.
Housekeeping	Sure, I will.

Conversation 5 Do Not Disturb

"Please hang up the 'Do Not Disturb' sign here."

Housekeeping	Hello? Housekeeping. May I come in?
Guest	Yes? What's the problem?
Housekeeping	May I come in to make up your room?
Guest	Oh, I'm sorry, but could you come back in two hours?
Housekeeping	Sure, sir. I'm sorry to disturb you. Next time, please hang up the 'Do Not Disturb' sign here.
Guest	Ok, I will. Well, can I get two face towels now?
Housekeeping	Sure. Here you are. When you need your room cleaned, please hang up the 'Make up Room' sign or call the operator.
Guest	Okay, thank you so much.
Housekeeping	You're welcome.

Conversation 6 Transferring a Request to Another Department

"I'll send someone in maintenance to your room"

Housekeeping	Good evening, ma'am. May I help you?
Guest	Oh, sorry. I forgot to take off the sign 'Do Not Disturb' Can I get turndown service right now?
Housekeeping	Certainly, ma'am. Is there anything you need?
Guest	Could you get me an extra blanket? It's cold in here.
Housekeeping	Of course. I will send someone with a blanket right away.
Guest	Oh, there is one more thing. The television doesn't work. There' s no sound coming from the TV.
Housekeeping	Is it plugged in?
Guest	Yes, it is. I already checked.
Housekeeping	I'm very sorry about that. I'll send someone in maintenance to your room, too.

Conversation 7 Delivering Laundry

"Where should I put your shirts and trousers?"

Housekeeping	Hello.
Guest	Who is it?
Housekeeping	Laundry service, sir. I have brought your laundry.
Guest	Just a moment, please. Come in.
Housekeeping	Where should I put your shirts and trousers?
Guest	Put them in the closet. There are lots of hangers in it.
Housekeeping	Would you sign the laundry slip, sir?
Guest	Sure, I will.

3. More Tips For You

Do Not Disturb (DND)

투숙객이 방해받고 싶지 않을 때, 호텔 객실에 직원의 출입을 금지한다는 표시로서 문에 걸어 두는 푯말이 있는데 이 푯말에 사용하는 문구가 'Do Not Disturb'입니다. 이 'Do Not Disturb' 푯말 뒷면에는 객실 정돈, 객실 청소를 요청하는 문구가 쓰여 있어 투숙객은 본인의 상황에 맞춰 푯말을 앞뒤로 사용하며 객실 문에 걸어 두면 됩니다.

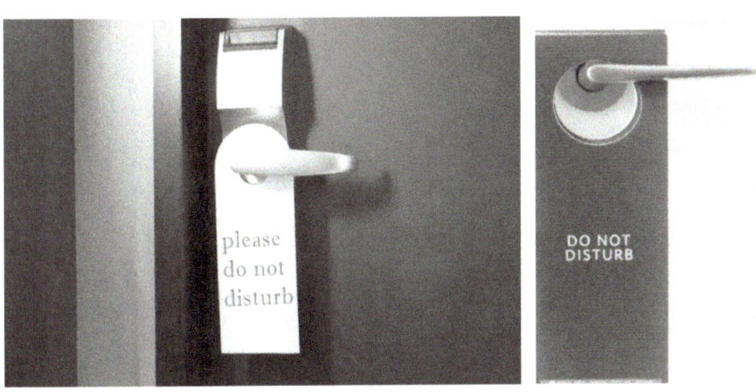

[객실에 걸려있는 Do Not Disturb 표지판]

그러나 최근 Do Not Disturb 관련 규정들을 바꾸는 호텔들이 늘어나고 있습니다. 일부 호텔들이 투숙객이 출입문 손잡이에 걸어놓을 수 있는 Do Not Disturb 표지판을 없애고 있는 것입니다. 예를 들어, 디즈니랜드 호텔을 포함한 디즈니사 소유 호텔들은 최근 'Do Not Disturb' 표지판을 모두 없애고 '방 안에 있음'(Room Occupied)이라는 표지판으로 모두 교체하였습니다. 디즈니 소유 호텔들에서는 문 앞에 'Room Occupied'라는 표지판이 걸려 있을 경우 청소 직원들은 들어가지는 않지만 대신 전문 교육을 받은 호텔 관계자가 객실 안에 무슨 일이 없는 지를 들어가 확인할 수 있습니다.

힐튼호텔 역시 Do Not Disturb 관련 정책을 변경하여 24시간 동안 룸 청소, 룸서비스 등 어떠한 서비스도 받지 않는 경우 호텔 측에서 고객이 투숙 중인 객실을 확인하도록 하고 있습니다. 물론 객실에 들어갈 때에는 반드시 노크를 하고, 객실에 들어가겠다는 것을 고객에게 알려야 합니다.

이처럼 호텔들이 Do Not Disturb 관련 정책들을 변경하고 기존 주기보다 짧아진 24시간 단위로 고객의 안전과 보안을 철저하게 살피는 이유는 지난 2017년 10월 1일에 미국 라스베이거스에서 발생한 총기 난사 사건의 영향이기도 합니다.

> The Disney Resort Hotel and its staff reserve the right to enter your room, even when this sign is displayed, for maintenance, safety, security or any other purpose. The Disney Resort Hotel staff will knock and announce their presence before entering.

[디즈니호텔 내 객실 'Room Occupied' 푯말 하단에 적힌 문구]

> We understand and respect your need for privacy. The hotel reserves the right to visually inspect all guest rooms every 24 hours to ensure the well-being of our guessts and confirm the condition of the room.

[힐튼 호텔의 'Do Not Disturb' 규정 관련 개정된 내용]

4. DIY

Can you explain these bedroom and bathroom objects?

Ⓐ

Ⓑ

Ⓒ

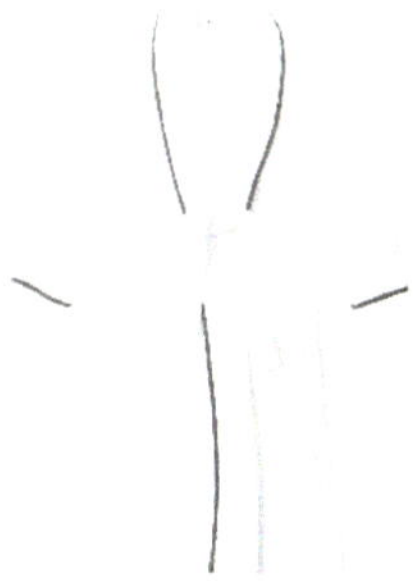

Ⓓ

Ⓔ

Ⓕ

A Story Behind the Hotel Brand

Shangri-La Hotels & Resorts
"아시아의 설탕 왕이 만든 무릉도원, 샹그릴라 호텔"

중국 푸저우 출신으로 말레이시아에서 사업을 시작하여 싱가포르, 홍콩, 인도네시아에 이르기까지 동남아 최대 그룹을 만들어낸 로버트 콱은 1947년 아버지가 세상을 떠난 후 다른 가족들과 함께 밀가루, 콩, 설탕 등을 유통하는 콱 브라더스를 설립하게 됩니다. 이후 1959년 로버트 콱은 일본인 두 명과 동업하여 제당회사를 설립하였는데 이 회사는 말레이시아 설탕시장을 독점하였고 1960년대 이후 그는 '아시아의 설탕왕'이 됩니다. 로버트 콱은 다양한 분야로 사업을 확장해 나갔고 1971년 싱가포르에 최초의 샹그릴라 호텔을 건설, 1977년에는 두 번째 샹그릴라 호텔을 홍콩에 설립합니다.

'샹그릴라'라는 호텔명은 1933년 제임스 힐튼의 소설 <잃어버린 지평선>의 무대였던 전설의 땅에서 유래하여 풍요롭고 평온한 무릉동원에 대한 동경과 함께 이와 같은 공간을 만들겠다는 포부를 담아 호텔명을 샹그릴라로 짓게 됩니다.
샹그릴라 호텔 앤 리조트 그룹 안에는 샹그릴라 뿐 아니라 케리(Kerry), 트레이더스(Traders), 젠(Jen) 등의 브랜드들이 포함되어 있고 2018년 1월 기준, 전 세계에 총 110개의 호텔을 보유하고 있습니다. 메인인 샹그릴라는 호화로운 시설에서 최고의 서비스를 제공하며 500실 이상 규모의 샹그릴라 호텔과 규모가 조금 더 작은 샹그릴라 리조트로 나뉩니다.
2011년에 탄생한 5성급 호텔 브랜드 케리는 최고의 서비스를 추구하는 젊은 비즈니스 고객을 주 타깃으로 하여 현대적으로 세련된 공간과 서비스를 제공하며, 1989년 등장한 트레이더스는 샹그릴라와 케리보다는 캐주얼한 컨셉의 중급 브랜드입니다. 젠은 가장 하위의 브랜드로서 기존 트레이더스를 젠으로 전환하는 작업을 진행 중에 있습니다.

샹그릴라에서 강조하는 '샹그릴라 호스피탈리티'란 사람을 생각하는 마음으로부터라는 이념으로 고객을 대하는 것으로서 마음에서 우러나는 최상의 서비스와 무릉도원에 있는 듯한 편안한 휴식을 제공하고 있습니다.

[Shangri-La Hotel Singapore]

[Shangri-La Hotel Paris]

[Shangri-La Resort Hainan]

[Shangri-La Resort Maldives]

[Traders Hotel Kuala Lumpur]

[Traders Hotel Abu Dhabi]

[Kerry Hotel Beijing]

[Kerry Hotel Shanghai]

[Hotel Jen Singapore]

[Hotel Jen Hong Kong]

Unit 10

Dealing with Complaints

We will learn
- how to deal with complaints
- how to apologize for mistakes
- how to find solutions

Hotel English

1. What They Do

고객으로부터 불평과 불만이 발생하였을 경우, 고객의 입장에서 원인과 과정을 정확하게 파악한 뒤 해결방안을 제시하여 신속한 대응을 해야 합니다. 구체적인 처리 요령은 다음과 같습니다.

- 진지한 표정과 진심어린 어조로 유감의 뜻을 표현합니다.
- 다른 고객과 분리된 장소로 옮겨 고객을 안정시킵니다.
- 고객의 불평과 불만에 대하여 공감하며 끝까지 경청합니다.
- 불평사항들은 메모를 하며 적극적인 자세로 대처합니다.
- 불평과 불만의 원인들을 파악하고 분석합니다.
- 고객의 요구사항을 신속하게 파악하여 고객의 뜻을 반영합니다.

고객 불평의 대표적인 유형에는 다음과 같은 내용들이 있습니다.

시설물 관련	온도, 조명, 미니바, 전자기기오작동, 객실 키, 불결함
서비스 관련	무례함, 불친절, 서비스 속도, 반응 속도, 서비스 오류 대기 시간, 수하물 서비스, 불결함, 음식 맛 불만
기타 불평	특정한 시설 부재에 따른 불만, 접근성, 교통, 운영시간

고객 불평의 재발을 방지하고 서비스 질을 향상시키기 위하여 고객 불평 내용들은 보고를 마친 후 다음과 같은 방법으로 기록해둡니다.

- Who (누가) - 불평의 주체
- When (언제) - 발생 시간
- Where (어디에서) - 발생 장소
- What (무엇을) - 불평 내용
- Why (왜) - 불평 발생원인
- How (어떻게) - 불평 처리 방법

2. Conversations

Conversation 1 Correcting Mistakes on the Bill

"I'm sorry for the inconvenience."

Guest Can I get my bill, please?

Olivia Yes, here it is.
Please check it over to find there is anything wrong.

Guest Oh, this isn't correct.
There is a room service charge for dinner here.
but I didn't have dinner in the room at all.

Olivia Let me check on the detailed bill, ma'am.
You were charged for sirloin steak, Ceaser's salad and onion soup.

Guest I just ate them in the restaurant on the second floor.
And I already paid at the restaurant after the meal

Olivia Oh, I see. Maybe the restaurant staff member made a mistake for requesting for the charge. I'm sorry for the inconvenience.

Conversation 2 Apologizing for Wrong Order

"I do apologize. I will exchange it at once."

John Here's your mineral water with lemon, sir.

Guest I think I can't drink out of that. The glass is dirty and there's lipstick around the edge. Please take it away and bring me another one.

John I'm very sorry, sir. I will replace it right away.

Guest Thanks.

John Here you are, sir. I hope this glass is better for you.

Guest Yes, that looks a lot better, but....

John Is there another problem, sir?

Guest I asked for still mineral water, not sparkling.

John Oh, sorry. I do apologize. I will exchange it at once.

Conversation 3 Moving Guests to a New Room

"Let me give you a new room."

Cindy Hello, Reception. May I help you?

Guest I just checked into room 1216, but this room has been already occupied by somebody. There is a luggage and a basket of fruit on the table. On the welcome card beside the basket someone else's name is written.

Cindy I'm really sorry for what happened. I'm wondering there must have been a mistake.

Guest That's Ok. So what should I do now?

Cindy Let me give you a new room.
Please stay in the room until our bellman comes up to your room. I'd like to give a complimentary wine as a small token of apology.

Guest Thank you.

Conversation 4 Solving Problems

"There's a problem with the air conditioning."

Operator Good morning. Operator. How can I help you, sir?

Guest My name is David Hamington in room 908.
There's a problem with the air conditioning.

Operator Please tell me in detail about it.

Guest I've just checked in. I can't turn it down and it's freezing in here. Also, the air conditioner sounds too loud.

Operator I'm sorry to hear that. I'll call Maintenance and have it fixed for you immediately.

Conversation 5 Explaining Situations

"I guess it happened we're very short-staffed tonight."

Guest Excuse me. We have some problems with our meals.

David Is there anything wrong, ma'am?

Guest My steak is supposed to be medium well done, but this is too overcooked.

David Oh, I'm really sorry that your steak is not cooked as you ordered. I guess it happened we're very short-staffed tonight. I'll take it back to the kitchen and get you another new one. It will be ready in about 15 minutes.

Guest And one more thing. I've been waiting for the wine waiter for 20 minutes.

David I do apologize, ma'am.
I'll send him to your table at once.

Guest Thank you.

Conversation 6 Apologizing for Mistakes

"She will make sure it doesn't happen again."

Henry Good morning. What can I do for you?

Guest This is Kelly Bright in room 725.
This morning I was woken up at 6 o'clock by a phone call. But it wasn't for me. I didn't request a wake up call. Now this is the second time.

Henry Oh, I'm terribly sorry for that.
I will inform the early morning operator.
She will make sure it doesn't happen again.

Guest Well, I hope not.

Conversation 7 Assist Guests in Need

"I will send a room attendant up to your room immediately."

Chloe Hello. How may I help you?

Guest I'm sorry, but my kids spilled milk over the bed.
And they knocked a glass of the table and broke it.
Of course I will pay for the damage when I check out.
Can you change the sheet and clean up the broken pieces?

Chloe Oh my gosh! Your kids are all right? Is there anyone to get hurt?

Guest Happily, they are fine.

Chloe Oh, good! What a relief!
I will send a room attendant up to your room immediately.

Guest Thank you very much.

Chloe You're welcome. If you need any help, just call us at anytime.

3. More Tips For You

Hotel Amenity

Amenity란 고객의 편의를 위하여 객실 내에 비치된 문구류, 객실용품, 욕실용품, 비품 등을 의미합니다. 다시 말하여 고객을 위하여 객실 내에 무료로 준비해놓은 각종 소모품 및 서비스 용품들을 일컫는 용어입니다. 호텔 어메니티는 단순한 물품의 의미를 넘어서서 호텔의 아이덴티티나 호텔의 격을 표현하는 중요한 수단이기도 합니다. 고급스러움을 강조하는 호텔의 경우, 아직 국내에 들어오지 않은 세계적인 명품 브랜드의 어메니티를 비치하여 객실의 품격을 표현하기도 하고 젊은 층을 주요 타깃으로 하는 트랜디한 호텔들의 경우에는 해외에서 주목받는 최신 브랜드의 어메니티를, 그리고 환경보호에 관심이 많은 호텔들은 친환경 브랜드의 어메니티를 사용함으로써 브랜드 이미지를 일치시키고 있습니다.

어메니티도 호텔 자산의 일부가 아닐까라는 생각에 호텔을 떠나며 어메니티를 챙겨 와도 될까 말까를 고민한 경험이 있을 테지만, 어메니티는 호텔에서 고객에게 무료로 제공되는 서비스의 일부이므로 어메니티를 챙겨오더라도 매너에 어긋나는 행동은 아닙니다.
메리어트 호텔 디자인 & 상품개발 부문 대표 스콧 미첼은
"고객이 어메니티를 챙겼다는 것은 고객이 호텔에 머문 것을 좋아했다는 것을 알 수 있는 시금석"이라고 언급했을 정도로 어메니티에 대한 고객들의 관심은 호텔에 대한 좋은 피드백으로 해석 가능하므로 최신 뷰티 브랜드의 제품도 사용해보고, 호텔에서 머물렀던 시간에 대한 기념품으로 간직하는 것도 호텔 이용의 즐거운 경험 중 하나입니다.

파크하얏트호텔 : 천연 식물성 원료만을 사용하는 호주 스킨케어 브랜드 [이솝]

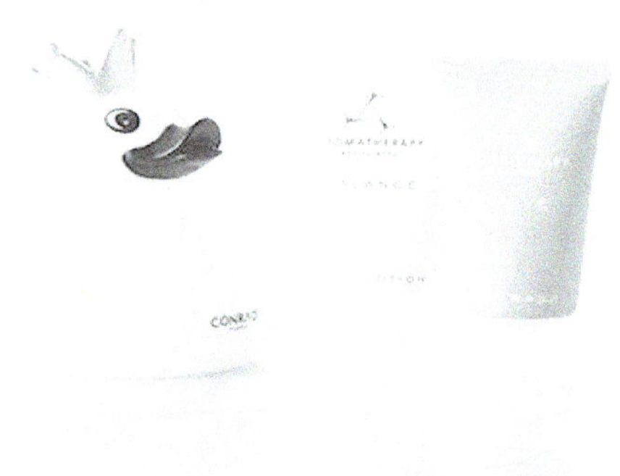

콘래드호텔 : 영국 황실에서도 사용하는 아로마 오일 전문 브랜드 [아로마테라피 어소시에이트]

신라호텔 : 영국 왕실에서 공식적으로 사용하는 배스 브랜드 [몰튼 브라운]

4. DIY

You made a mistake in this morning and the guest expressed strong dissatisfaction. You passed on the guest's complaint and the General Manager sent the guest an email. Complete the words in the email below.

Dear Mr. Thompson,

I am s__________(1) to hear that your stay in our hotel wasn't

completely satisfactory. I a__________(2) that your were disturbed

late at night.

Next time you stay with us p_________(3) contact me directly and

I will arrange for you to be upgraded to s__________(4).

Our suites are on a quiet f__________(5) and I am sure you

w__________(6) be very comfortable.

I look f__________(7) to welcoming you back to the hotel soon.

Yours sincerely,
Caroline Brown
General Manager

A Story Behind the Hotel Brand

The Peninsula Hotel
"수에즈 운하 동쪽에 최고의 호텔을!"

홍콩에서는 더 펜(the Pen)이라는 애칭으로 잘 알려진 페닌슐라 호텔은 홍콩의 대표적 랜드마크이자 세계 10대 호텔 중 하나입니다.

1919년 시베리아 횡단열차의 완성으로 홍콩을 방문하는 유럽 부자들이 증가할 것이라는 예측하고 1928년 '수에즈 운하 동쪽에 최고의 호텔을' 이라는 목표 아래 홍콩에 첫 번째 페닌슐라 호텔이 탄생하게 되었고 이 호텔은 홍콩 최고의 럭셔리 호텔로 자리 잡게 됩니다.

페닌슐라 호텔은 유례없는 호화로움과 서비스를 제공합니다. 특히 1970년 이래로 롤스로이스사 차량을 고객 서비스 전용으로 사용하고, 2006년에는 롤스로이스 팬텀 14대를 한꺼번에 인도하여 화제가 되기도 하였습니다. 1994년 원래의 건물과 같은 디자인의 30층 타워가 세워졌으며 옥상에는 헬기 이착륙장이 있습니다. 호텔은 스위트룸과 일반객실을 포함하여 모두 300개의 객실이 있고 호텔보다 더 유명한 페닌술라 스파와 고대 로마풍의 수영장, 식당 등을 갖추고 있습니다. 오후 2시가 지나면 라운지 'The Lobby'의 대표적인 상품인 애프터눈 티를 즐기기 위한 사람들로 북적입니다. 티파니 식기에 담긴 정통 영국식 애프터눈 티는 투숙객만 예약이 가능하기 때문에 예약을 할 수 없는 일반 방문객들은 페닌슐라만의 애프터눈 티를 즐기기 위해 늘 긴 줄을 기다려야만 합니다. 아케이드에는 80여 개의 명품숍이 있어 홍콩의 쇼핑장소로도 알려져 있습니다.

지금은 홍콩 이외에도 뉴욕, 시카고, 베버리힐스, 방콕, 베이징, 마닐라, 도쿄, 상하이, 파리에서 페닌슐라 호텔을 만날 수 있습니다.

페닌슐라 호텔의 철학 중 하나는 전통을 이어나가는 것입니다. 80년 넘는 역사를 지닌 페닌슐라 호텔은 각 호텔이 위치한 도시와 국가의 전통과 문화를 적절히 가미시켜 최고급 서비스를 제공하고자 합니다.

객실에 들어서면 전담 버틀러가 따뜻한 중국 전통차를 내오며 “Welcome to the Peninsula!”라고 인사하는 대목이나 페닌슐라 방콕에서는 가슴 앞으로 두 손을 모으고 인사하는 태국 전통 인사법인 ‘와이’식으로 고객에게 인사하는 것 역시 전통을 중시하는 그들만의 가치관을 엿볼 수 있는 부분입니다.

페닌슐라 호텔 레이니 챈 총지배인은 다음과 같이 말합니다.
“더 펜은 왕관과 같습니다. 왕관은 우리 기업, 그리고 9개의 호텔은 왕관에 박힌 반짝이는 보석과도 같습니다. 홍콩이 다이아몬드라면 방콕은 루비이며 뉴욕은 에메랄드라고 할 수 있습니다. 저마다의 개성과 아름다움이 존재합니다. 시대의 흐름에 맞춰 서비스 수준은 높여가지만 전통은 바꾸지 않습니다. 바꿀 필요가 없죠. 그것이 더 펜이니까요.”

[The Peninsula Hotel]

[Peninsula's Rolls-Royce Service]

[Peninsula's Afternoon Tea Set]

Unit 11

Giving Directions

We will learn
- how to give directions
- how to offer guests information
- how to explain each place clearly

Hotel English

1. What They Do

호텔리어의 기본 역할은 고객들이 원할 때 언제든지 정확한 정보와 서비스를 제공하는 것입니다. 각종 관광정보, 주변 식당, 쇼핑 시설 안내, 교통편, 각종 행사 및 공연 정보 등에 대한 정보들을 제공할 수 있어야 합니다. 어떤 정보 요청에도 신속하게 대응할 수 있도록 지도 및 안내서, 팸플릿 등을 구비하는 것은 기본이며 준비한 자료만으로는 정보 전달이 부족할 경우 인터넷을 활용하여 실시간 업데이트된 정보들을 제공하여 안내하도록 합니다. 필요시 관련 부서와의 원활한 협조를 통하여 고객이 필요로 하는 바를 빠른 시간 내에 얻을 수 있도록 도움을 주며 필요에 따라 예약까지 진행합니다.

길 안내 시에는 현재 호텔의 위치를 지도에 표시한 뒤 고객이 원하는 목적지까지 가는 최상의 방법을 안내합니다. 도보, 대중교통, 택시 등을 이용하여 목적지까지 가는 방법 안내와 함께 소요 시간 및 비용, 기타 유용한 팁들을 함께 상세히 안내하여 고객이 목적지까지 어려움 없이 도달할 수 있도록 돕습니다. 다양한 정보들은 수시로 변화하므로 항상 최신 정보들을 수집하고 있어야 하며 고객들의 눈에 잘 띄도록 로비 스탠드에 각종 관광 안내 책자 등을 비치해둡니다.

2. Conversations

Conversation 1 To the Bank

"There are lots of banks on Oxford Street, which isn't far away."

Daniel Good afternoon, ma'am. How can I help you?

Guest I've just checked in and I don't have any local currency. Is there an ATM in the hotel?

Daniel I'm sorry. We don't have it in the hotel but there are lots of banks on Oxford Street, which isn't far away.

Guest Could you show me where it is?

Daniel Sure. Let me give you a map of the city. The hotel is here. I'll circle it for you. Oxford Street is about 10 minutes' walk away.

Guest How can I get to Oxford Street?

Daniel Turn left out of the hotel. Walk along the street and turn right at the traffic lights. Walk along Baker Street and then turn left onto Oxford Street. There are lots of banks there with ATM.

Guest That's very clear. Thank you very much.

Daniel My pleasure, ma'am.

Conversation 2 To the Traditional Market

"They are the most typical traditional markets in Seoul."

Guest Good evening. I need to buy some souvenirs for my colleagues. I want to buy them in a Korean traditional market. Is there any place near here?

Daniel Of course, sir. There are Namdaemun Market and Dongdaemun Market. They are the most typical traditional markets in Seoul.

Guest Oh, really? Very interesting. I want to visit both of them. What is the best way to get there?

Daniel I'd like to recommend taking the subway.
This is a map of Seoul, and the back is a map of the subway. You can find the subway station when you turn left as soon as you go through the hotel's revolving door.

Guest Thanks a lot. I'm so excited.

Conversation 3 To the Room

"Actually that's at the other end of the corridor."

Guest Excuse me. I'm looking for my room.

Emily May I have your room number, please?

Guest Yes, my room number is 158.

Emily Actually that's at the other end of the corridor.
Follow me, please. I'll show you to your room.

Guest Thank you so much. It's very kind of you.

Emily It's my pleasure to serve you.
And watch your steps, please. The floor is wet.

Guest Ok, thank you.

Conversation 4 To the Fitness Center

"Go through the door past the information desk and go down the stairs."

Guest Could you tell me how to get to the fitness center?

Calvin It is in the basement.
Go through the door past the information desk and go down the stairs. Go along the way and turn left.
And the fitness center is in front of you.

Guest Thank you so much.

Conversation 5 To the Gift Shop

"Well, it is over there behind the bakery past the lobby."

Guest	Excuse me, is this the right way to the gift shop?
Celine	I'm afraid it isn't.
Guest	Oh, no. And How can I get there?
Celine	Well, it is over there behind the bakery past the lobby.
Guest	I see. Thank you.
Celine	You know.

Conversation 6 To the Airport

"Are you going to the international or the domestic airport?"

Guest My plane leaves at 6 o'clock. How long does it take to get to the airport by taxi?

Mark Are you going to the international or the domestic airport?

Guest International.

Mark The traffic is very heavy at that time.
I think you need to be there at least two hours in advance.
So you had better take the 3 o'clock shuttle.

Guest Where can I catch the shuttle?

Mark In front of the hotel.

Guest Thank you. I'll take it.

Conversation 7 To the Department Store

"If you go by bus, it takes about 25 minutes."

Guest	Can you recommend a department store to do some shopping?
Jake	Most big stores are in downtown.
Guest	What's the best way to get there?
Jake	If you go by bus, it takes about 25 minutes. And the subway takes less time.
Guest	I will take the subway. Where is the subway station?
Jake	It isn't far from the hotel. You go out of the hotel and turn left. It's within a five-minute walk.
Guest	I appreciate it.
Jake	You're very welcome. My pleasure.

Conversation 8 To the Hair Salon

"Go across the lobby and through that doorway."

Guest Excuse me. How can I find the hair salon?
I'd like to get my hair trimmed before the conference.

Michell It's on the ground floor. Go across the lobby and through that doorway. Turn to the left and it's at the end of the corridor.

Guest Can I have my hair dyed there as well?

Michell Of course, you can, ma'am.

Guest Sounds perfect!

3. More Tips For You

Hotel Classification

호텔 등급을 구분하는 방법은 나라마다 차이가 있습니다. 일반적으로 유럽에서는 별로 등급을 표시하고 최고 등급의 호텔은 별 5개 호텔입니다. 미국에서는 다이아몬드로 등급을 구분하기도 합니다.

우리나라는 1970년에 호텔 등급을 4등급으로 운영하였고 이후 1986년 12월 31일자로 관광사업법이 '관광진흥법'으로 개정되면서 관광진흥법시행령 제22조에 의거하여 관광호텔업의 등급을 특1급, 특2급, 1등급, 2등급, 3등급 등 5개로 나누었으며 등급은 무궁화로 표시하였습니다.

2015년 문화관광체육부는 한국관광공사를 '호텔업 등급결정 사업'의 주관 기관으로 지정하여 한국관광공사는 2015년 1월 1일부터 별 등급 제도를 도입하였고, 관광진흥법시행령 제22조에 의거 호텔업의 등급을 5성급, 4성급, 3성급, 2성급, 1성급으로 나누며 '별'로 등급을 표시하기 시작하였습니다. 5성급은 별 5개, 4성급은 별 4개, 3성급은 별 3개, 2성급은 별 2개, 1성급은 별 1개로 표시됩니다.

호텔업 등급결정은 문화체육부장관이 따로 정하여 고시한 호텔업 등급평가기준에 의하여 결정되며 5성급은 90% 이상, 4성급은 80% 이상, 3성급은 70% 이상, 2성급은 60% 이상, 1성급은 50% 이상의 점수를 획득하여야 인정받게 됩니다.

호텔 등급 기준

★	깨끗한 객실, 욕실, 조식 가능, 안전
★ ★	1성급 + 최소한의 식음료 부대시설
★ ★ ★	2성급 + 1개 이상의 레스토랑, 로비, 라운지
★ ★ ★ ★	고급스러운 시설과 서비스, 품격 있는 로비, 품위 있는 가구, 높은 품질의 침구, 연회장, 국제회의장, 비즈니스센터, 피트니스센터, 2개 이상의 레스토랑, 룸서비스 12시간 이상 가능
★ ★ ★ ★ ★	최상급 시설과 서비스, 4성급 시설 + 3개 이상의 레스토랑, 룸서비스 24시간 가능

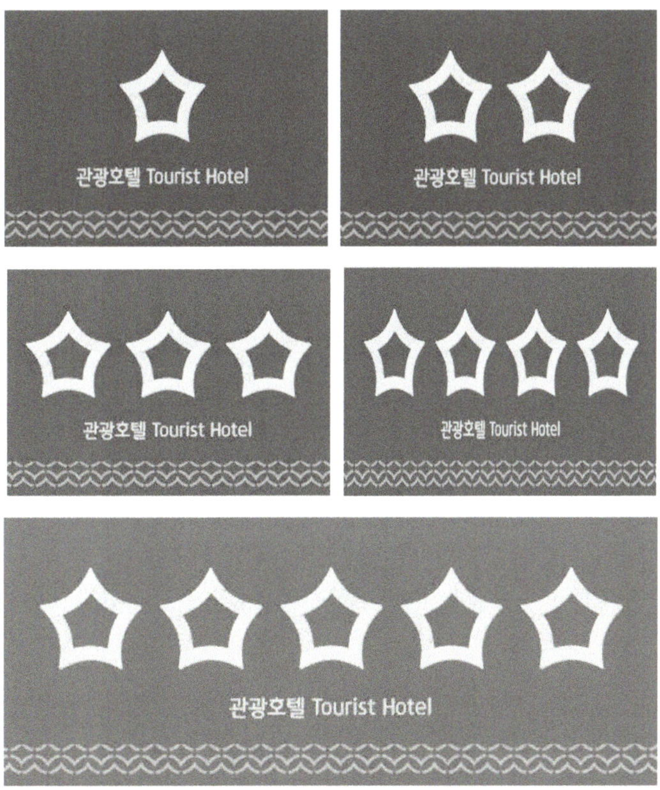

4. DIY

Look at the map and tell guest how to get to the places

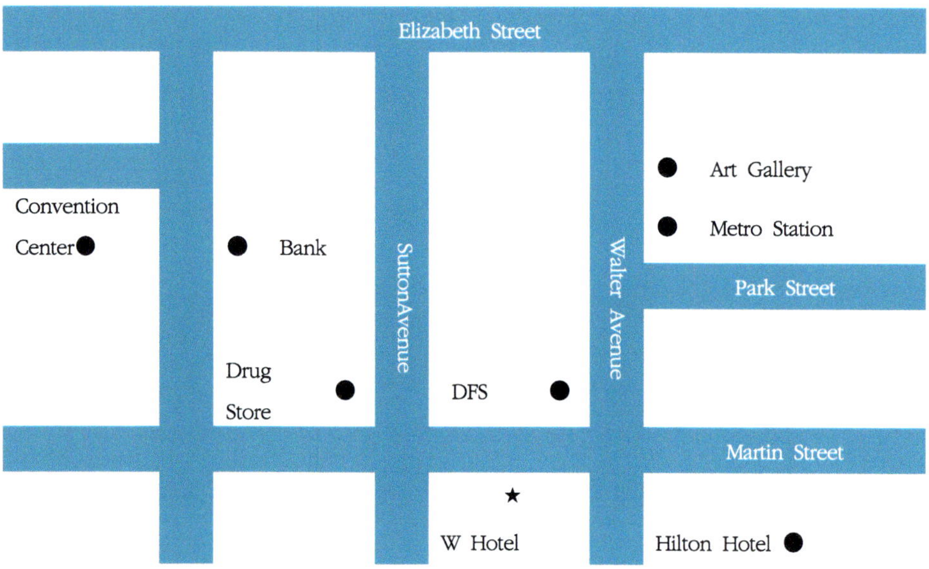

(1) Can you tell me how to get to the convention center?

(2) I need some medicine. How can I get to the drug store?

(3) Excuse me, where's art gallery?

(4) I can't find park street. Can you help me with this map?

(5) Is there another hotel nearby?

A Story Behind the Hotel Brand

Mandarin Oriental Hotel
"오리엔탈리즘과 모더니즘의 융합"

만다린 오리엔탈 호텔 그룹의 모회사는 홍콩의 자딘 매디슨(Jardine Matheson)사입니다. 자딘 매디슨은 1832년 영국 동인도회사 소속 의사이던 윌리엄 자딘(William Jardine)과 제임스 매디슨(James Matheson)에 의해 광저우에 세워진 회사로 중국 이름은 이화양행(怡和洋行), 또는 사전양행(渣甸洋行)입니다. 동인도회사의 대중국무역 독점이 폐지된 1834년 자딘매디슨은 '사라(Sarah)'라는 이름의 선박으로 영국에 홍차와 비단을 수출하였고, 인도산 아편을 수입하여 중국에 수출함으로써 많은 부를 축적하게 됩니다. 1963년 자딘 매디슨은 홍콩섬 무역 금융 중심지인 콘노트 로드에 첫 번째 호텔 만다린 오리엔탈 호텔 홍콩(Mandarin Oriental Hotel Hong Kong)을 개관하였습니다. 만다린 오리엔탈 호텔 홍콩은 오랜 시간 아시아 최고의 호텔로 인정받으며 홍콩 섬의 전설적인 호텔로 자리 잡게 되었고 수많은 세계 명사들이 선호하는 호텔이기도 합니다.

만다린 오리엔탈 호텔은 아직 국내에 들어오지 않은 호텔 브랜드이지만 우리나라에서도 화제가 된 사건이 있었습니다. 홍콩의 유명 가수 장국영이 2003년 4월 1일 만다린 오리엔탈 호텔 홍콩 24층 객실에서 투신하여 세상을 떠났고 그가 떠난 지 9시간 만에 홍콩에서는 6명의 팬이 투신하여 5명이 자살하는 사건들까지 이어지는 등 홍콩 본토뿐만 아니라 전 아시아권의 영화팬들이 그의 죽음을 애도하였습니다. 많은 세월이 흐른 지금도 해마다 그의 기일인 4월 1일에는 그를 기억하는 세계 각국의 팬들이 호텔 앞에 모여 그를 추모하고 있습니다.

만다린 오리엔탈 하이드파크 런던(Mandarin Oriental Hyde Park London)은 1889년 오픈하여 영국 왕실을 비롯한 영국 상류층의 사교 공간으로 사랑받고 있습니다. 만다린 오리엔탈 하이드파크 런던에는 영국 왕실과 관련된 이색적인 패키지 상품들이 눈길을 끕니다.

호텔 내에는 왕실과 연관된 일을 전담하는 '로열 앰버서더'라는 전문 직원이 있으며 2011년에는 윌리엄 왕세자와 케이트 해밀턴의 결혼식을 기념하며 왕실 웨딩 투어 상품을 내놓기도 하였습니다. 왕실 결혼식이 열리는 웨스트민스터 사원과 컨싱턴 궁 등 왕실과 관련된 역사적 명소들을 둘러보고 특별석에 앉아 결혼식 및 퍼레이드를 관람할 수 있으며, 스펜서 가와 처칠 가에서 백작과 함께 식사와 티타임을 즐길 수 있는 체험 상품입니다. 2012년에는 엘리자베스 여왕 즉위 60주년을 맞이하여 '다이아몬드 주빌리 투어'를 출시하기도 하였는데 이 상품은 퍼레이드를 특별석에서 관람하며 왕가 사저를 방문하고 처칠 가에서 점심 식사를 즐기는 4박 5일 프로그램으로 이상의 두 개의 상품 모두 영국 왕실과 호텔이 연계한 유일한 상품이라는 점에서 다소 높은 가격임에도 큰 인기를 끌었습니다. 2018년 기준 만다린오리엔탈호텔그룹은 아시아, 미국, 유럽, 중동, 아프리카 등 21개국에 30개의 호텔과 6개의 레지던스를 운영 중이며 각 도시 및 국가의 문화와 정서를 반영하며 만다린 오리엔탈만의 특색 있는 호텔들을 세계 곳곳에 확장 중에 있습니다.

[Mandarin Oriental Hotel Hong Kong Suite Room]

[Mandarin Oriental Hotel Bangkok]

[Mandarin Oriental Residence Boston

Unit 12

Business Service

We will learn
- how to explain available services
- how to provide equipment
- how to support guest's business works

Hotel English

1. What They Do

비즈니스센터는 고객들의 각종 비즈니스 업무를 수행하는데 필요한 다양한 장비와 공간 및 서비스를 제공하는 부서입니다.
비즈니스 센터의 대표적인 업무는 다음과 같습니다.

- 비서 업무의 수행
- 팩스, 복사, 프린트 업무
- PC, Laptop 제공 및 Wifi 서비스
- 회의실 제공 및 회의 준비
- 행사 예약과 진행
- 우편물 및 택배 취급 서비스
- 각종 이용현황 작성 및 보고
- 업무 체크리스트 점검
- 각종 업무의 번역 및 통역
- 고객의 불편사항 처리

비즈니스센터는 다음의 3가지 요소들이 매우 중요합니다.

① 접근성
비즈니스센터가 로비에 위치할 경우 접근성이 용이한 반면, 다소 산만하여 업무 집중도가 떨어질 수 있습니다. 반면 로비를 제외한 다른 층에 위치할 경우 접근성은 다소 떨어지더라도 방해받지 않고 차분한 분위기에서 업무를 볼 수 있다는 장점이 있습니다.

② 최신 기자재

기기나 프로그램을 최신 버전으로 업데이트하고, 첨단 장비들을 갖춤으로써 비즈니스 고객들의 다양한 업무활동을 지원할 수 있어야 합니다.

③ 전문성

비즈니스센터는 '사무실을 떠난 사무실'(office away office)의 개념이므로 담당 직원은 업무의 기능성과 서비스성을 모두 갖추고, 다양한 비즈니스 고객의 업무를 명확하게 숙지하고 전문성을 갖춰야 합니다.

2. Conversations

Conversation 1 Fax Service

"Where can I fax this?"

Guest	Where can I fax this?
Reception	Would you mind going to the Business Center? They're in charge of FAX.
Guest	Thank you.
Reception	You're welcome.

(in the Business Center)

Business Center	Good afternoon. May I help you?
Guest	Could you fax this for me?
Business Center	Certainly. Where to, sir?
Guest	Two pages to Chicago. The number is 1-206-389-7634. Would you charge it to my room?
Business Center	Please tell me your name and your room number, sir.
Guest	Michael Brown, 1206.
Business Center	Please sign this bill, Mr. Brown.
Guest	Ok. Thank you.

Conversation 2 Photocopy Service

"Can you tell me how I can make some photocopies?"

Business Center Good morning. What can I do for you?

Guest Can you tell me how I can make some photocopies?

Business Center Sure. You can either leave it with Reception and we'll organize that for you or you can do it yourself here.

Guest I'll do it myself here. Then how do I pay for it?

Business Center You can either pay directly here or charge it to your account

Guest Will you charge it to my account?

Business Center All right, sir.

Conversation 3 Printing Service

"we can print them and deliver them to your room."

Business Center	Good morning. Business Center. May I help you?
Guest	I printed some documents in my e-mail at the Business Center. But they are foo faint. The print machine seems to need more toner.
Business Center	I'm sorry to hear that. If you send us the files, we can print them and deliver them to your room. Our e-mail address is thehotel@gmail.com
Guest	That sounds great. Let me send the files right away.
Business Center	Your copies will be delivered within 20 minutes.
Guest	Perfect! Thank you very much.

Conversation 4 Parcel Service

"We provide three types of international mail express services"

Guest	Can I send this package to Australia?
Business Center	Sure. What are there in the box?
Guest	There are 3 books and some canned food for my son.
Business Center	Is there anything fragile inside?
Guest	No, there isn't.
Business Center	We provide three types of international mail express services : DHL, FedEx and EMS. Which service would you like?
Guest	I will send it by EMS.
Business Center	Would you like to purchase insurance for 10 dollars?
Guest	No, thank you.
Business Center	There is a handling charge of 20 dollars. How would you like to pay it?
Guest	Will you put it on my room bill, please?
Business Center	All right, sir. I'll do that.

Conversation 5 E-mail Service

"I need to check my e-mails"

Business Center	Good Evening. Can I help you?
Guest	Hi. Is this the business center? I need to check my e-mails
Business Center	Yes it is, sir. Are you staying at the hotel?
Guest	Yes. I'm in room 1242
Business Center	The business center is free for guests, sir
Guest	Can I use the printer here, too?
Business Center	Yes, you can, but there is a charge
Guest	How much does it cost?
Business Center	It costs 2 dollars per sheet
Guest	Can I charge it to my room?
Business Center	Yes, of course

Conversation 6 Meeting Room Service

"When would you like to use the meeting room?"

Business Center	What can I do for you?
Guest	We're planning a meeting for eight people. Can I reserve a meeting room?
Business Center	Of course, you can. We have a room for eight people. When would you like to use the meeting room?
Guest	Tomorrow from 9 a.m. to 4 p.m. What about audio-visual equipment? We are going to have a presentation there.
Business Center	The meeting room has free wireless Internet access. We can also organize digital projectors and screens. And you can rent laptop computers.
Guest	That sounds perfect. Will you arrange 8 personal laptops?
Business Center	Absolutely, sir. Please write your name and your room number here.

3. More Tips For You

EFL (Executive Floor)

비즈니스센터 업무와 중복되는 부분도 있는 호텔 내 EFL (Executive Floor)에 대해 더 살펴보겠습니다.
EFL은 호텔 내 VIP 전용층으로 호텔 내 작은 호텔(A Small Hotel Within a Hotel)로서 호텔의 일반 VIP 고객과 VIP 비즈니스고객들을 대상으로 호텔 내 모든 서비스를 제공하는 곳입니다. 이곳에 투숙하는 이용객들에게는 익스프레스 체크인, 익스프레스 체크아웃, EFL 라운지와 피트니스클럽 무료이용 등의 혜택들이 제공되고 외국어 및 업무가 능숙한 전문 플로어 매니저가 상주하며 다양한 업무를 지원하고 있습니다. EFL 이용객들은 단골고객 및 VIP 고객이므로 사전에 고객의 기호나 특성, 요청사항 등을 꼼꼼히 확인하고 최상의 서비스를 제공할 수 있도록 각별히 주의를 기울일 필요가 있습니다.
대부분의 5성급 호텔들은 호텔의 가장 전망 좋은 고층에 특정 층을 지정하여 EFL을 운영 중이며 숙련된 직원들을 배치하고 간단한 음료와 주류, 간식 등을 무료로 제공하기도 합니다.

[서울신라호텔 EFL 라운지]

4. DIY

Complete the conversation between the person in charge of business center and the guest using the items below

Ⓐ 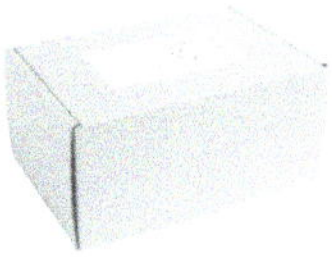

Ⓑ 

Ⓒ 

Ⓓ 

A Story Behind the Hotel Brand

InterContinental Hotel
"항공사에서 탄생한 브랜드"

1946년 4월 4일 팬 아메리칸 월드 항공사(Pan American World Airways)는 첫 번째 호텔 브랜드를 출시하였고 그 브랜드가 바로 인터컨티넨탈 호텔입니다. 당시 남미와 태평양 노선을 이용하는 승객과 승무원을 위한 숙박 시설로 시작하였으나 1970년대 유가 폭등, 미국 항공 자유화로 인한 요금 경쟁 등의 위협요인으로 경영난에 시달리게 됩니다. 여러 회사들에 매각되고 재인수되는 과정들을 거쳐 1998년 영국의 맥주 회사 바스(Bass)에 매각되었습니다. 1989년 당시 영국 정부가 양조가들이 직영하는 술집의 수를 제한하자 바스는 호텔사업으로 눈을 돌리며 북미를 중심으로 사업을 확장해나가기 시작했습니다. 2000년 양조 자산을 '바스'라는 이름과 함께 벨기에의 양조회사 '인터브루(Interbrew)'에 넘기고 '식스 컨티넨트사(Six Continents plc)'로 사명을 바꾸었으며, 2003년 4월 인터컨티넨탈 호텔 그룹(InterContinental Hotels Group)을 설립하여 그룹 내 호텔 브랜드로 인터컨티넨탈 호텔 앤 리조트(InterContinental Hotels and Resorts), 홀리데이 인(Holiday Inn), 캔들우드 스위트(Candlewood Suites), 스테이브릿지 스위트(Staybridge Suites), 크라운 플라자(Crowne Plaza) 등이 있습니다. 이렇게 항공사에서부터 그 역사가 시작된 인터컨티넨탈 호텔은 항공사가 취항하는 대부분의 도시에서 만나볼 수 있을 정도로 거대 호텔 기업으로 성장하게 되었으며, 인터컨티넨탈 호텔 특유의 서비스 감각은 이코노미클래스부터 퍼스트클래스까지 다양한 고객층을 만족시키는 항공사 서비스로부터 영향을 받은 것으로 보입니다. 현재 전 세계 100여 개국에 5,000개 이상의 호텔과 약 744,000개의 객실을 보유한 인터컨티넨탈 호텔 그룹은 IHG 리워드 클럽(IHG Rewards Club)이라는 호텔 멤버십 프로그램을 운영 중으로, 인터컨티넨탈 브랜드 호텔에서 미화 1달러를 사용할 때마다 10포인트가 적립되어 포인트 숙박이나 제휴사 쇼핑, 항공 마일리지 전환 등이 가능하게 함으로써 브랜드 충성도를 높이고 있습니다.

[2017년에 오픈한 InterContinental Ljubljana Hotel]

[2014년 IHG가 인수한 미국의 부티크 호텔 그룹 Kimpton]

[중국 고객들을 위하여 만들어진 IHG 그룹의 새로운 브랜드 HUALUXE]

Unit 13

Checking-out

We will learn
- how to check guests out
- how to prepare the bill for a guest
- how to say goodbye to guests

Hotel English

1. What They Do

체크아웃은 투숙객이 호텔 객실과 식음료 및 기타 부대시설 이용 요금에 대한 지불을 마치고 호텔을 떠나는 것을 의미합니다. 고객과 접촉하는 마지막 순간이기도 하므로 고객에게 좋은 인상으로 남아 재방문을 유도할 수 있도록 신속하고 효율적인 업무처리를 해야 합니다.
체크아웃은 다음과 같이 분류됩니다.

- 일반 체크아웃
- 익스프레스 체크아웃
- 단체 체크아웃
- 후불고객 체크아웃
- 레이트 체크아웃

일반적인 체크아웃 과정은 다음과 같습니다.

① 인사 - "고객님, 안녕하십니까?"
② 객실 키 건네받고 객실번호의 고객과 체크아웃 고객의 확인
"네 1214호 김지연 고객님 맞으십니까?"
③ 불편사항 체크 - "불편하신 점은 없으셨습니까?"
④ 미니바 사용여부 확인 - "객실 미니바에서 사용하신 품목 있으십니까?"
⑤ 요금지불방법 문의 - "요금은 체크인 때 사용하셨던 카드로 지불하시겠습니까?"
⑥ 폴리오 출력 - "내역 확인 부탁드리겠습니다."
⑦ 환송인사 - "저희 호텔을 이용해주셔서 감사합니다. 다음에 또 뵙겠습니다. 안녕히 가십시오."

2. Conversations

Conversation 1 Checking Guests Out

"I hope you enjoyed your stay at this hotel."

Guest	I'd like to check out now.
Front Desk	Sure, ma'am. May I have your name, please?
Guest	My name is Jennifer Watson.
Front Desk	What was your room number?
Guest	Room 1752
Front Desk	How was your stay, Ms. Watson?
Guest	It was really great, thank you.
Front Desk	Are you using the same credit card you gave me when you checked in?
Guest	Yes, that's right.
Front Desk	Ok, Ms. Watson. Please check this print out : two nights' accommodation, breakfast on Sunday morning, room service on Friday night, five international phone calls.
Guest	Yes, they're all correct
Front Desk	Will you sign here, please? Thank you. Would you like me to staple your credit card slip to your bill?
Guest	Yes, please. And here are my key cards
Front Desk	Thank you, here is your receipt, Ms. Watson. I hope you enjoyed your stay at this hotel.
Guest	Definitely, very much. Goodbye!
Front Desk	Goodbye, ma'am.

Conversation 2 Checking the Bill

"Please look it over if everything is correct."

Front Desk Good morning. May I help you?

Guest We're checking out now. We were in room 507. Here are two keys for the room.

Front Desk Yes, wait a moment. Did you have anything from the minibar while you were staying at the hotel?

Guest Yes, we had three bottles of mineral water and two chocolate bars.

Front Desk Ok. I will add those to your bill. Let me print your bill. Could you sign here, please?

Guest Here you go.

Front Desk Thank you, sir. Here is your bill. Please look it over if everything is correct.

Conversation 3 Payment

"How would you like to pay?"

Guest	Excuse me. We're leaving now.
Front Desk	Would you like to check out now?
Guest	Yes, please. My room number is 1502. Here is my key.
Front Desk	Thank you. How was your stay with us?
Guest	It was excellent.
Front Desk	Let me print your bill. Here you go. How would you like to pay?
Guest	By credit card, please. Here it is.
Front Desk	I'm sorry, but your card was declined. Do you have another one?
Guest	Oh, really? Do you take Master Card?
Front Desk	Yes, we do. We accept all major credit cards.

Conversation 4 Late Check-out

"Can I stay in my room until late this afternoon?"

Front Desk Good afternoon, sir. Can I help you?

Guest Good afternoon. I'm supposed to leave today, but my flight departs at 00:40 tomorrow.
Can I stay in my room until late this afternoon?

Front Desk Let me check if the room is available first.
Yes, the room is available tonight.

Guest That's good. Until when can I check out?

Front Desk Until 6 p.m. sir. But you'll get an additional charge for late checkout. The late checkout fee is 40 dollars.

Guest I see. Thank you for your kindness.

Front Desk You're welcome.

Conversation 5 Organizing a Taxi

"Will you call me a taxi to the international airport?"

Front Desk	Good morning. Front Desk. What can I do for you?
Guest	Will you send someone to take my luggage to the front. I'm going to check out at 10 o'clock.
Front Desk	How many pieces of luggage do you have?
Guest	I have two suitcases and two bags.
Front Desk	Yes, sir. The bellman will be there in a minute.
Guest	Thanks. And will you call me a taxi to the international airport? I have to arrive at the airport by noon.
Front Desk	Yes, sir. Let me tell you when the taxi is ready. Please wait in the lobby.
Guest	Thank you.
Front Desk	Did you enjoy your staying at our hotel?
Guest	Certainly. It was a great weekend. I'm sure I'll be back.
Front Desk	We hope to see you again, sir. Have a safe trip.

Conversation 6 Preparing the Bill

"Will you prepare my bill while I am having breakfast?"

Front Desk Good morning. Are you checking out?

Guest Yes. Will you prepare my bill while I am having breakfast? Here is my key.

Front Desk All right, sir.

Guest Is my bill ready?

Front Desk Yes, sir. Here is your bill.
Is there anything wrong on the bill?

Guest Everything looks fine. Can you make two separate bills for me? My company will only pay for the room and the meals, and I should pay for the extra services.

Front Desk Sure, sir. Here they are.

Guest Great! Let me pay with my Visa card.

Front Desk Thank you. Here are your separate bills and receipts.

Guest It's very nice of you.

Front Desk You're welcome. Have a nice trip back home, sir.

3. More Tips For You

Tipping Policy

팁 문화의 시작은 18세가 영국에서 시작되었습니다. 당시 영국의 한 펍(Pub)에 '신속하고 훌륭한 서비스를 위해 지불을 충분하게'라는 문구가 붙어 있었습니다. 후에 이 문구는 'To Insure Promptness'(신속함을 보장받기 위하여)로 간소화되었고 이것의 머리글자를 따서 팁(Tip)이 되었습니다. 팁은 제공받은 서비스에 대한 대가이자 감사의 표현이지만 우리나라에서는 아직 익숙하지 않은 문화이기도 합니다. 그럼에도 불구하고 팁 문화가 정착된 나라를 여행할 때에는 때와 장소에 맞게 적절한 팁을 건네는 것이 에티켓입니다. 호텔에 투숙하게 되면 객실을 정돈해주는 룸 메이드에게 1달러 정도의 팁을 침대 베개에 놓고 방을 나오는 것이 일반적이며 이를 베드팁이라고도 합니다. 호텔 로비에서 문을 열어주며 환영해주는 도어맨에게는 굳이 팁을 주지 않아도 되지만, 만약 도어맨이 차에서 무겁고 많은 짐을 내려주었다면 1~2달러 정도를 건네는 것이 좋습니다. 도어맨을 거쳐 호텔 로비에서 객실까지 짐을 옮겨주는 벨맨에게는 보통 가방 한 개당 1~2달러 정도의 팁을 건네는 것이 보편적이며 만약 체크아웃할 때 벨맨을 따로 불러서 짐을 옮겨야 한다면 체크인 때와 마찬가지로 가방 한 개당 1~2달러를 건네면 됩니다. 프론트데스크 직원에게는 따로 팁을 건네지는 않지만 만약 컨시어지 부서에 까다로운 서비스를 요청했다면 감사의 표시로 조금 더 넉넉한 팁을 건네는 것이 좋습니다. 호텔 F&B 업장 내에서 음료나 식사를 주문할 시에도 팁을 지불해야 하며, 만약 영수증에 음식 값 외에 별도의 봉사료가 포함되어 있다면 따로 팁을 주지 않아도 무관합니다.

[호텔 팁(Tip) 문화]

4. DIY

Put the words in the sentences into the correct order

(1) was room what number your?

→ ____________________

(2) have the you anything minibar did from?

→ ____________________

(3) you stay did enjoy your?

→ ____________________

(4) please here you sign could?

→ ____________________

(5) the card same you are credit using?

→ ____________________

A Story Behind the Hotel Brand

Hotel Shilla
"영빈관에서 시작된 역사"

호텔신라의 역사는 영빈관에서부터 시작됩니다. 영빈관은 1959년 이승만 대통령이 국빈용 숙소를 따로 지으라는 지시를 내리면서 계획된 장소로 4·19혁명과 5·16군사정변을 거치면서 두 차례 공사가 중단되었다가 1967년 완성되었습니다. 정부는 1973년 경영난에 빠졌던 국영 워커힐 호텔과 영빈관을 민간 기업에 팔기로 결정하였고 그 가운데 서울 장충동 영빈관은 삼성그룹 초대회장인 이병철 회장의 뜻에 따라 1973년 삼성이 인수하면서 호텔신라의 역사가 시작되었습니다. 1973년 5월 9일 주식회사 임페리얼로 회사를 설립하고 1973년 11월 호텔기공식을 시작으로 서울시 중구 장충동에 공사를 진행하여 1979년 3월 8일 호텔 전관을 개관하며 천년 역사와 함께 가장 찬란한 문화예술의 꽃을 피웠던 신라 왕조의 이름을 따라 호텔신라의 명칭을 사용하여 현재에 이르고 있습니다. 호텔신라는 1986년 신라면세점 서울점을 열고 면세점 사업에 뛰어들기 시작하였으며, 1990년 제주신라호텔을 오픈하게 됩니다. 서울이 품격을 강조한 도심 속 고품격 호텔 컨셉이라면 제주신라호텔은 자연과 잘 어우러진 고급 리조트 호텔 컨셉으로 제주의 사계절을 다 담아낼 뿐 아니라 글램핑 시설까지 갖추고 있습니다.

개관 이래 품격 높고 차별화된 서비스를 바탕으로 세계 각국의 수반과 명사들로부터 찬사를 받아온 호텔신라는 서울 올림픽 본부 호텔, IOC 서울총회, FIFA 공식 VIP호텔, 다보스 세계 경제 포럼 등 세계적 행사들을 치러내며 대한민국을 대표하는 호텔로서 그 위상을 높이고 있으며, 2002년부터 세계 정상의 여행 전문지인 미국의 자갓 지(Zagat誌), 트래블 앤 레저 지(Travel & Leisure誌)와 콘데 나스 트래블러 지(Conde Nast Traveler誌), 최고 권위의 금융 전문지 인스티튜셔널 인베스터 지(Institutional Investor誌) 등 세계 유수의 매체들로부터 높은 위상을 인정받고 있습니다.

호텔신라는 안주하지 않고 시장의 흐름에 맞춰 2013년 실용성을 강조한 비즈니스 호텔 브랜드인 '신라 스테이'를 선보였고 2013년 11월 동탄점을 시작으로 현재 11개의 신라스테이를 운영 중에 있습니다.
호텔신라의 오랜 숙원 사업 중 하나는 도심 속에 한옥호텔을 오픈하는 것입니다. 호텔신라 이부진 사장은 취임 이후부터 제대로 된 한옥호텔을 짓겠다는 의지를 보여 왔지만 한옥호텔 건립은 쉽지 않았습니다. 호텔신라의 한옥호텔은 서울시 심의를 통과하는 데만 5년이 걸려 2016년에야 사업안을 승인받을 수 있었기 때문입니다. 서울시는 자연경관 훼손, 문화경관 보호 등의 이유로 반려와 보류 등 한옥호텔 건립을 부결시켰지만 그때마다 호텔신라는 지적사항을 모두 개선하며 강력한 의지를 보여 왔습니다. 이 과정에서 호텔신라는 한옥호텔의 건축 규모를 당초 지상 4층에서 지상 2층으로 줄이기도 했습니다. 처음부터 쉽지 않은 사업이었고 수차례 난항을 겪고 있지만 만약 계획대로 2022년 호텔신라의 새로운 한옥호텔이 성공적으로 완공된다면 우리나라 호텔업계에 새로운 반향을 일으킬 것으로 예상됩니다.

[Hotel Shilla Seoul]

[Shilla Stay Haeundae in Busan]

[Shilla Hanok Hotel Plan]

Unit
14

Payment

We will learn
- how to understand payment procedure
- how to check guest's bill accurately
- how to correct mistakes on the bill

Hotel English

1. What They Do

지불은 보통 체크아웃 시에 이루어지며 이때 고객이 숙박하는 동안 발생된 미불금액을 회수하거나 결제방법을 선택하고 정확한 객실판매기록표를 작성하여 고객에 대한 기록을 남겨놓습니다.
객실을 이용하는 동안 발생되는 대표적인 요금에는 다음과 같은 것들이 있습니다.

- 객실요금 (Room Charge)
- 식음료업장요금 (F&B Charge)
- 비즈니스센터요금 (Business Center Charge)
- 전화이용요금 (Telephone Charge)
- 세탁요금 (Laundry Charge)
- 미니바 이용요금 (Mini Bar Charge)
- 유료채널시청요금 (Pay TV Charge)

이와 같은 공표요금 외에 상황에 따라 특별요금들이 추가되거나 할인되는 경우도 있습니다.

- comp : 무료를 뜻하는 complimentary의 약자로 VIP고객이나 호텔에 큰 기여를 한 고객들에게 무료로 객실을 제공하기도 합니다.
- 할인 : 비수기나 주중 이용객, 사전예약고객, 단체이용객들에게는 일정 비율 이상의 할인율을 적용하여 객실을 판매하며, 투숙객들은 호텔 내 시설들을 이용시 할인혜택을 받기도 합니다.
- 추가 : 체크아웃 시간을 넘기거나 고객의 요청에 의해 체크아웃을 연장하는 경우 추가요금이 부과되며 추가로 침대를 요청하거나 객실 내 기물을 파손할 경우에도 별도의 요금을 지불해야 합니다.
- 봉사료와 세금 : 팁 문화가 정착되지 않은 우리나라의 경우 객실이나 식음료에 대하여 일률적으로 10%의 봉사료를 청구하고 있습니다.

2. Conversations

Conversation 1 Separate Payment

"How would you like to split your bill?"

Guest	Excuse me, my friend and I are going to split the bill. Can we have the check, please?
Brandon	Of course, let me help you with that. How would you like to split your bill?
Guest	We will each pay half by credit card. How much is the bill?
Brandon	The total amount will be $124 including tax, sir. Would you like me to help you with the payment now?
Guest	Yes, with these cards please.
Brandon	Sure, I'll be right back with your receipts.
	(Few moments later)
Brandon	Thank you for waiting. Here are your cards and receipts. The payment has been completed. Is there anything else I can help you with?
Guest	No, that will be all. Thank you.

Conversation 2 Confusion Regarding Bill

"Excuse me, I think this bill isn't correct."

Guest Excuse me, I think this bill isn't correct.
Can you check this for me?

Maria Sure, of course. May I see your bill?
Let me double check for you, ma'am.
One moment, please.

Guest Ok, I will be back in 5 minutes.
Is that enough time for you?

Maria Yes, I think 5 minutes will be plenty.

(5 minutes later)

Guest I'm back. What was the issue with the bill?

Maria Ma'am, I've checked the details and you have stayed for 4 nights with us. The laundry service has been used 2 times by your room number. Is this right?

Guest Yes, I remember but I thought it was a complimentary service because I have a membership at this hotel.

Maria No, ma'am. Unfortunately, the laundry service is not included as free of charge service with the membership.

Guest Oh, I see. Maybe I should go through the service list again.
Thank you anyway.

Maria You're welcome. Have a good day and thank you for staying with us.

Conversation 3 Tipping Policy

"Please keep the change."

Tony　That's 57.25 dollars, Mr. Hong.
How would you like to pay?

Guest　I will pay by cash. But I need to go to the ATM machine first. Is there an ATM machine in the hotel?

Tony　Yes, there is one on the first floor. You can take the elevator down, take a left and you will see the ATM at the end of the corridor.

Guest　Ok, I will be right back.
How much was it again?

Tony　It is 57.25 dollars, sir.
Are you ready to make the payment?

Guest　Yes, here you go.

Tony　Thank you, one moment, sir.
And I'll get you your change.

Guest　No, that's alright. Please keep the change.

Tony　Thank you I really appreciate it but unfortunately there is no tipping policy at our hotel.

Conversation 4 Payment System Error

"I'm sorry, but I see no previous records of completed payment."

Eileen Are you checking out, sir?

Guest Yes, but can I leave my bags for 30 minutes?

Eileen Sure, let me help you with the checking out first.
Here is your bill. How would you like to pay?

Guest Excuse me? I've made all the payments online when I booked the hotel.

Eileen I'm sorry, but I see no previous records of completed payment.
Can you show me the online receipt?
Or perhaps the proof of completed payment on your reservation site.

Guest I booked on Expedia. Here is the receipt.

Eileen Great. Could you please give me some time to check with someone from Expedia?

Guest Yes, please check and let me know.

Eileen Sir, I've checked with Expedia and I believe there has been a system error on all payments made online yesterday. Your payment status has been correctly adjusted. I'm very sorry for your inconvenience.

Guest No worries. I'll be back to get my bags later.

Conversation 5 Additional Payment

"You will have to pay additional 450 USD."

Shelly: Good afternoon, welcome to Conrad Hotel, how can I help you today?

Guest: Hello, I've made a reservation for a standard type room but I would like to upgrade the room to a suite for tonight.

Shelly: Okay, may I have your name and the reservation number please?

Guest: My name is Ben and here is the reservation number.

Shelly: Great, I will first check the availability for the suite room. Sir, fortunately there is one available tonight but the room is city view. All ocean views are fully booked. Is this okay for you?

Guest: Yes, I suppose. Then how much more do I need to pay?

Shelly: You will have to pay additional 450 USD. Should I proceed with the upgrade?

Guest: Yes, please. Here is my credit card.

Shelly: Your room upgrade has been completed, sir. Your room number is 3607 and here is your key card. On your receipt, your previous reservation for the standard room tonight will have been revised but if not, please speak to us at the front desk.

Guest: Perfect! Sounds good. Have a good one.

Conversation 6 Currency Exchange

"I'd like to exchange U.S. dollars for Korean currency."

Guest I'd like to exchange U.S. dollars for Korean currency, please. What's the rate today?

Kelvin Today's exchange rate is 1,116 won to U.S. dollars.

Guest Great, can you also check the exchange rate for Yen?

Kelvin Sure, today's rate is 1,015 Won to Yen.

Guest Okay then could I please exchange 100,000 won to U.S. dollars and 50,000 to Yen?

Kelvin How would you like your bills sir?

Guest Could you please give me all the dollars in 10 dollar bills and Yen in 100?

Kelvin No problem, may I please have your passport and your room number?

3. More Tips For You

계산, 날짜, 환율, 객실 번호 등 다양한 숫자들을 영어로 읽는 방법에 대하여 구체적으로 살펴보겠습니다.

① 객실 번호는 영어로 어떻게 표현할까요?

객실번호는 일반적으로 세 자리 숫자나 네 자리 숫자로 이루어져 있습니다. 객실 번호를 읽는 방법은 일반적인 숫자 읽는 방법과 마찬가지로 두 자리씩 끊어서 말하는 것이 원칙이나 세 자리 숫자의 객실은 한자리씩 끊어서 간편하게 말하기도 합니다.

- 객실 번호 829호 = eight twenty nine
- 객실 번호 707호 = seven oh seven
- 객실 번호 2862호 = twenty eight sixty two
- 객실 번호 1407호 = fourteen oh seven / fourteen seven

② 시간은 영어로 어떻게 표현할까요?

- [정각] The time is 4 o'clock / It's 4 o'clock
- [15분] 4시 15분 : It is a quarter past 4
- [30분] 4시 30분 : It is half past 4
- [45분] 4시 45분 : It is a quarter to 5

③ 전화번호는 영어로 어떻게 표현할까요?

전화번호는 각각의 숫자를 한자리씩 끊어서 읽으면 됩니다.

566-2786 = My phone number is five six six two seven eight six

④ 분수와 소수는 영어로 어떻게 표현할까요?

분수는 분자 → 분모 순으로 읽고 분모는 서수로 말해야 합니다.

- 1/3 = one-third
- 2/3 = two-thirds
- 2/1 = one-half
- 1/4 = one-quarter

소수점은 point라는 단어를 사용하나 돈의 경우에는 dollars와 cents를 사용하여 읽습니다.

- 52.23 = fifty two point twenty three (fifty two point two three)
- $52.23 = fifty two dollars (and) twenty three cents
- 98.19 = ninety eight point nineteen (ninety eight point one nine)
- $98.19 = ninety eight dollars (and) nineteen cents

⑤ 돈을 셀 때는 영어로 어떻게 표현할까요?

- 천원 = one thousand won
- 만원 = ten thousand won
- 십만 원 = one hundred thousand won
- 백만 원 = one million won

USD ($)			KEW (₩)		
100	One hundred	백달러	100,000	One hundred thousand	십만원
1,000	One thousand	천달러	1,000,000	One millon	백만원
10,000	Ten thousand	1만달러	10,000,000	Ten million	천만원
1000,000	One hundred thousand	10만달러	100,000,000	One hundred million	일억원
1,000,000	One millon	100만달러	1,000,000,000	One billion	십억원
10,000,000	Ten millon	1000만달러	10,000,000,000	Ten billion	백억원
100,000,000	One hundred millon	1억달러	100,000,000,000	One hundred billion	천억원
1,000,000,000	One billion	10억달러	1,000,000,000,000	One trillion	1조원
10,0000,000,000	Ten billion	100억달러	10,000,000,000,000	Ten trillion	10조원
100,000,000,000	One hundred billion	1000억달러	100,000,000,000,000	One hundred trillion	100조원

4. DIY

Practice checking-out procedure and handling a confusion regarding payment with the given guest folio

FOLIO

DATE	DETAILS	TOTAL
31-Jan	Room Rate	134.00
31-Jan	Tax 1	2.68
31-Jan	Tax 2	10.12
31-Jan	Room Service	21.50
31-Jan	In Room Movie	10.00
01-Feb	Room Rate	134.00
01-Feb	Tax 1	2.68
01-Feb	Tax 2	10.12
01-Feb	Laundry Service	15.00
02-Feb	Room Rate	134.00
02-Feb	Tax 1	2.68
02-Feb	Tax 2	10.12
02-Feb	Mini Bar	22.37
02-Feb	Room Service	52.00
	Total Charges	561.27

A Story Behind the Hotel Brand

Lotte Hotel
"만인의 연인, 샤롯데"

Lotte라는 명칭은 괴테의 명작 <젊은 베르테르의 슬픔>에 나오는 여주인공 '샤롯데'에서 따온 이름입니다. 샤롯데는 전 세계 독자들에게 사랑받는 '만인의 연인'으로 롯데그룹은 샤롯데와 같이 만인에게 사랑받는 기업이 되고자 그 아름다운 여성의 이름을 그룹명으로 짓게 됩니다.

1914년 남대문, 서울역과 가까운 소공동은 경성의 새로운 중심지로 떠오르기 시작하였고 이때 개관한 조선호텔은 그 중심이 되어 국빈, 고위관리, 외국 유명 인사들이 투숙하는 최고급 호텔로 자리 잡게 됩니다.

어느 날 일본의 신흥 부자 노구치 시타가우(野口遵)가 조선호텔에 투숙하기 위해 호텔로 들어섰지만 그의 남루한 옷차림 때문에 호텔 투숙을 거부당하는 사건이 생기고 이에 큰 모멸감을 느낀 노구치는 1938년 조선호텔 바로 옆에 지상 8층의 반도호텔(현재 롯데호텔 자리)을 짓고 꼭대기 층 집무실에서 조선호텔을 바라보며 맺힌 한을 풀었다는 일화가 있습니다. 이렇게 탄생한 반도호텔은 1973년 롯데그룹이 (주)호텔롯데을 세우며 반도호텔을 인수하였고, 1979년 호텔롯데은 반도호텔을 완전히 헐고 지상 38층, 1000개의 객실, 18개의 레스토랑을 보유한 '롯데호텔서울'을 새로 선보였습니다.

이후 롯데호텔 부산, 롯데호텔 울산 등이 잇따라 탄생하게 되고 현재 롯데호텔은 우리나라에 5개, 미국에 2개, 러시아에 4개, 베트남에 2개, 미얀마에 1개의 호텔을 운영 중입니다. 이 외에도 브랜드를 확장하여 럭셔리 브랜드 시그니엘과 비즈니스 관광객을 위한 롯데시티호텔, 그리고 트랜디하고 감각적인 라이프스타일 호텔 브랜드 L7까지 선보이며 다양한 고객들을 유치하고자 지속적으로 변화를 시도 중에 있습니다.

국내 브랜드 가운데 최다 호텔 체인을 운영 중인 롯데호텔은 2018년 9월 1일 서울 명동에 이그제큐티브 타워(EX)를 오픈하기도 하였습니다. 서울 강남에 롯데시그니엘이 있다면 강북에는 EX타워가 있는 셈입니다. 롯데호텔서울 EX타워는 타 경쟁호텔들과 차별화를 두기 위하여 특색 있는 서비스들을 선보이고 있고 특히 로열스위트룸은 41억 원을 투자하여 완성한 국내 최대 규모(140평, 460.8㎡)라는 점에서 이슈가 되고 있기도 합니다.

[1938년 반도호텔]

[Lotte Hotel Seoul]

[Lotte Hotel Russia]

[Lotte Hotel Executive Tower Royal Suite Room]

호텔용어 A-Z

A

Adjoining Room 인접해있는 객실

Advance Deposit Guarantee 고객이 도착하기 전 일정금액을 예치하도록 하는 예약보증의 한 형태

All Inclusive 호텔에서 제공하는 식사 및 부대시설을 추가 비용 없이 이용할 수 있는 서비스

Amenity 투숙객의 편의를 위해 객실에 무료로 배치하는 물품으로 일회용 욕실용품과 슬리퍼, 각종 사무용품 등을 의미

American Breakfast 커피와 티, 주스, 빵, 과일, 베이컨 등에 계란요리가 곁들여진 미국식 아침 식사

American Plan 객실요금에 아침, 점심, 저녁 식사가 포함되는 요금제도

Aperitif 식욕촉진효과가 있는 식전주

Appetizer 전채요리

Arrival Time 고객 등록 카드 등에 기록하는 고객이 호텔에 도착한 시간

Ashtray 재떨이

B

Baggage Tag 수하물에 소유자를 표시한 꼬리표

Ball Room 대연회장

Banquet 연회

Bermuda Plan 객실에 미국식 조식이 포함된 호텔 숙박요금 제도의 일종

Blocked Room 단체, 국제회의참석자, VIP 등을 위해 사전에 객실을 지정해 놓는 것

C

Cancellation Charge 고객의 일방적인 취소에 따른 예약취소 수수료

Catering 식음료 부서에서 담당하는 일종의 출장요리

Charge, Tariff 요금

Check Room 호텔에서 고객의 내용물을 보관해 주는 장소

Closet 옷장

Commercial Rate 특정 기업이나 일부 비즈니스 고객에게 일정 비율로 할인을 해 주는 것

Complimentary 객실 내 무료로 제공되는 식음료

Concierge 투숙객이 원하는 다양한 요구와 정보를 제공해주는 서비스

Confirmation Slip, Confirm Sheet 예약확인서

Connecting Room 객실과 객실 사이에 문이 연결된 객실

Continental Breakfast 커피와 티, 주스, 빵 종류만으로 구성된 유럽식 아침 식사

Crip, Baby Bed 어린이 투숙객을 위한 유아용 침대

Cuisine 요리, 요리법

Cutlery 테이블에서 사용하는 나이프, 포크, 스푼 등과 같은 은기류

D

Decanting 와인을 마시기 전 침전물을 없애기 위해 다른 깨끗한 용기(Decanter)에 와인을 옮겨 따르는 것

Deposit 호텔 내 기물파손 등 비용이 발생되는 상황을 대비하여 보증금을 내는 것

Dine Out 전문 식당 등에서 외식하는 것

Discount Group Rate 단체고객을 유치하기 위한 할인 제도

DND (Do Not Disturb) 객실에 종업원의 출입을 금지한다는 방해금지 표시카드로서 투숙객이 직접 객실 문에 걸어둘 수 있다.

Door Open Service 투숙객이 열쇠를 분실하거나 별도의 고객 요청에 의하여 마스터 키로 문을 열어주는 서비스

Down Grading 호텔 객실 사정으로 예약 받은 객실 가격보다 저렴한 가격으로 고객을 객실에 투숙시키는 것

Dump 고객이 지정된 예약날짜나 시간보다 미리 체크아웃 절차를 받는 것

Duty Manager 밤 시간대부터 그 다음날 오전까지 근무하는 당직 지배인

E

Early Check-in 규정시간보다 이른 시간에 체크인 하는 것

Estimated Time of Arrival 고객의 도착 예정 시간

Estimated Time of Departure 고객의 출발 예정 시간

European Plan 객실비와 식사비를 분리하여 각각 별도의 계산을 하는 요금제도

Exchange Rate 환율

Executive Floor 최고의 서비스를 제공하는 호텔 내 귀빈층

Extra Charge 기본요금 외에 부과되는 추가 요금

F

FB (Full Board) 호텔에 투숙하는 동안 아침, 점심, 저녁 모든 식사 제공

Finger Food 손으로 집어먹을 수 있는 작은 크기의 음식

Folio 투숙객이 호텔을 이용하는 동안 사용한 비용명세서

Foreign Exchange Rate 외환율

Full House 모든 객실이 100% 모두 판매된 상태

G

Garnish 음식이나 음료에 얹거나 뿌리는 장식

Go Show 호텔의 빈 객실(Vacant Room)이 없을 경우에 체크-인(Check-In) 예정 고객 중 예약취소나 No-Show(노쇼)로 빈 객실을 구하려고 기다리는 고객

Guest History Card 고객 방문 기록 카드

H

Happy Hour 호텔 식음료 업장에서 고객이 붐비지 않은 특정 시간대에 저렴한 가격 또는 무료로 음료 및 스낵 등을 제공하는 호텔 서비스

HB (Half Board) 아침과 점심, 또는 아침과 저녁식사 두 끼의 식사 제공

House Phone 호텔 로비에 놓인 구내 전용전화

House Use Room 호텔 임원이나 직원이 객실을 사용하고 있음을 나타내는 객실 상황 표시

I

In Order Room 호텔 객실의 정리정돈이 완료되어 판매를 할 수 있는 객실

In Season Rate, Peak Season Rate 수요가 급증하는 성수기 요금

Inside Call 호텔 내선 전화

Inventory 재고조사, 재고관리

J

Join Us Charge, Extra Charge 체크인 이후 추가 인원이 머물 경우 부과되는 추가요금

L

Late Arrival 예약시간보다 늦게 도착한 고객

Late Check-out 규정시간보다 늦은 시간에 체크아웃 하는 것

Laundry 투숙객 세탁물, 직원 유니폼 세탁, 외부 수주 세탁물 등 모든 세탁업무

Linen Room 하우스 키핑을 지원하기 위한 린넨 보관 장소

Lost and Found 분실물 보관소

M

Make-Up 투숙객이 체류하는 동안 침대의 린넨을 교환하거나 객실을 청소하고 정돈을 하는 것

Make Up Card 투숙객이 객실 청소를 요청하는 표시로 객실의 문에 걸어 놓는 카드

N

No-Show 예약한 고객이 당일에 호텔에 나타나지 않는 것

Numbering Stand 연회행사나 컨벤션 시각 테이블마다 표시한 번호

O

Occupancy Rate 호텔 객실 이용률

Occupied (객실을) 사용 중인

Off-Season Rate 비수기에 공표요금에서 할인해 주는 비수기 요금

On Change Room 고객이 체크아웃을 하였으나 아직 객실청소가 완료되지 않은 객실

Open Bed 고객이 베드에 들어가기 쉽도록 베드 스프레드를 벗기고 단정하게 접어놓는 서비스

Order Slip 서버가 작성하는 식음료 주문전표

Order Taker 식당이나 객실에서 주문을 받는 사람

Out Of Order 사고나 객실 보수 등의 사유로 고객에게 판매가 불가능한 객실

Outside Call 호텔 외부에서부터 걸려오는 전화

Over Booking 초과예약

P

Permanent Guest 장기체류고객

Pressing Service 런드리에서 담당하는 고객 세탁물의 다림질 서비스

R

Receipt 영수증

Registration 숙박등록

Registration Card 숙박등록카드

Reservation Confirmation 예약 확인

Rooming 입실

Room Inspection 객실 청소와 정리가 종료된 후 고객에게 객실을 판매하기 전에 최종적으로 객실을 점검하는 것

Room Rate 객실요금

Room Service 고객의 요청으로 호텔 객실에서 하는 식사 서비스

S

Service Charge 봉사료

Sewing Kit 반짇고리

Shift 호텔 종사원의 근무조 또는 근무시간

Skipper 호텔, 레스토랑, 기타 부대시설의 요금을 지급하지 않고 몰래 떠나는 고객

Sleep Out 객실료를 지불하였으나 객실에서 숙박하지 않고 외부에서 숙박한 고객

Split '반병, 반잔'이란 뜻으로 1Split은 16온스를 말한다.

Stationery 호텔객실 비품 가운데 문구류로 봉투, 편지지, 엽서, 볼펜 등을 말한다

Suite Room 욕실이 딸린 침실 한 개와 거실 겸 응접실 한 개 등으로 구성된 2실 이상 연속 객실

T

Tariff 요금표

Traveler's Check 여행자 수표

Turn Down Service 투숙객의 취침 직전에 제공하는 서비스로써 간단한 객실의 청소·정리·정돈과 잠자리를 돌봐 주는 작업

V

Vacancy 판매 가능객실이 아직 남아 있는 상태

VAT (Value Added Tax) 부가가치세

Voucher 고객의 호텔 예약 증명서류로 체크인 시 제출하면 된다.

W

Wake-Up Call 사전에 투숙객의 요청을 받은 교환원이 고객의 객실로 전화벨 신호로 잠을 깨워 일어날 시간을 알리는 것

Walk in Guest 사전에 예약을 하지 않고 당일에 직접 호텔에 와서 투숙하는 고객

Walk Out 투숙객이 공식적인 체크아웃 절차를 거치지 않고 호텔을 떠나는 경우

Will Call for Service 투숙객이나 호텔을 출발할 고객이 외부인에게 물품을 전달할 경우에 물품 보관 후 외부 손님에게 전달하는 서비스

Wine Taste 와인 시음

저자 소개

양제연

경희대학교 영어영문학 학사
경희대학교 일반대학원 호텔관광학 석사
경희대학교 일반대학원 호텔관광학 박사
University of California, Berkeley Extension 수료
San Jose State University Extension 수료
전) CID 관광 마케터 및 개발 컨설턴트
현) 두원공과대학교 호텔관광과 교수
Director of International Partnerships, Univ. of Philippines
(사)오페라마 예술경영연구소 연구위원
한국호텔관광학회 정회원
한국관광레저학회 정회원
파주시 축제자문위원회 위원
파주시 적극행정 지원위원회 위원

Hotel English

2019년 2월 15일 초 판 1쇄 발행
2021년 2월 20일 제2판 1쇄 발행
2024년 4월 15일 제2판 3쇄 발행

지은이 양제연
펴낸이 진욱상
펴낸곳 (주)백산출판사
교 정 편집부
본문디자인 오행복
표지디자인 오정은

저자와의 합의하에 인지첩부 생략

등 록 2017년 5월 29일 제406-2017-000058호
주 소 경기도 파주시 회동길 370(백산빌딩 3층)
전 화 02-914-1621(代)
팩 스 031-955-9911
이메일 edit@ibaeksan.kr
홈페이지 www.ibaeksan.kr

ISBN 979-11-6567-243-0 13740
값 19,000원